EDUCATION AND SOCIAL JUSTICE IN A DIGITAL AGE

Rosamund Sutherland

First published in Great Britain in 2014 by

Policy Press
University of Bristol
6th Floor
Howard House
Queen's Avenue
Clifton
Bristol BS8 1SD
UK
t: +44 (0)117 331 5020
f: +44 (0)117 331 5367
pp-info@bristol.ac.uk
www.policypress.co.uk

North America office:
Policy Press
c/o The University of Chicago Press
1427 East 60th Street
Chicago, IL 60637, USA
t: +1 773 702 7700
f: +1 773 702 9756
sales@press.uchicago.edu
www.press.uchicago.edu

British Library Cataloguing in Publication Data
A catalogue record for this book is available from the British Library

Library of Congress Cataloging-in-Publication Data
A catalog record for this book has been requested

ISBN 978 1 44730 524 8 paperback
ISBN 978 1 44730 525 5 hardcover

The author and publisher would like to thank Tim Soar for permission to reproduce the
photograph on page 77.

Policy Press works to counter discrimination on grounds of gender, race, disability, age and
sexuality.

Cover design by Andrew Corbett
Front cover photos: vintage slate chalk board – ViFi/Bigstock;
tablet – bloomua/Bigstock
Printed and bound in Great Britain by CPI Group (UK) Ltd,
Croydon, CR0 4YY

Policy Press uses environmentally responsible print partners.

Contents

About the author

Rosamund Sutherland is Professor of Education at the Graduate School of Education, University of Bristol, UK. Her research has been concerned with teaching and learning with ICT (information and communications technology), young people's use of digital technologies outside school and mathematics education. She has led a wide range of research projects funded by the Economic and Social Research Council, and collaborated with colleagues in Latin America, Europe and Africa. In this book she brings together the previous strands of her research, with a particular focus on social justice.

Acknowledgements

This book has been inspired by my work as a governor of Merchants' Academy in South Bristol, and I am indebted to all the people who are contributing to the success of this school, including teachers, parents, governors and the young people themselves. I would particularly like to thank Denis Burn who chaired the project board that set up the school and was the first Chair of Governors. It was under Denis's leadership that the educational vision of the school was established, the beautiful new school was built and the challenges of the long-term enterprise were recognised. I would also like to thank the current Principal, Anne Burrell, for showing me what it means to embrace the endless challenges involved in school leadership, and the first Principal, Stephen Kings, who recognised the importance of the University of Bristol as a sponsor of the school, working alongside the Society of Merchant Venturers. The commitment of the governors is staggering and I have learned so much from working with Chris Curling (the current Chair of Governors), Lynn Robinson, Lucy Collins, Chris Willmore, Richard Morris, Peter McCarthy, Laura Marshall and David Crawford.

Whereas my work as a governor grounds me, my work as an academic enables me to see things differently by engaging with theory, literature, data and debate. All of this academic work is influenced by conversations and collaborations with colleagues. For this reason I am indebted to everyone who has influenced my thinking and writing over the years. In particular I would like to thank Nicolas Balacheff, Sally Barnes, Laurinda Brown, Anna Edwards, Martine Duggan, Keri Facer, John Furlong, Marina Gall, Demetris Lazarou, Elizabeth McNess, Federica Olivero, Noreen O'Loughlin, Andrew Pollard, Teresa Rojano and Wan Ching Yee. I also wish to thank Sarah Eagle, John Morgan and Michael Young for reading drafts of the book and providing me with both invaluable feedback and encouragement to finish.

I owe a huge debt to Alison Shaw, the Director of Policy Press for suggesting that I write the book, and then nudging me through the process and understanding my way of working. I also wish to thank Laura Greaves who managed the final stages of editing so that this was both pleasurable and productive. As always Mary O'Connell has provided me with support whenever I needed it, and so thank you Mary for being there ever since I came back to Bristol as an academic in 1995.

Finally this book would never have been finished without the love and support of my husband Ian, who always understands when I need to escape to write and never stops believing in me. He has been beside me throughout my long journey as an academic and makes sure that I keep a balance in my life between adventure and mindfulness.

Preface

In writing a book about social justice and education I have chosen to focus on the importance of knowledge in the curriculum. And I am aware that sometimes people talk about knowledge and education as somehow being in opposition to play, happiness and freedom. Even as I write this preface the incoming chair of the association that represents the elite private schools in the UK[1] has criticised the government for developing a curriculum that neglects the wider needs of education, arguing that children's happiness is being sacrificed by the focus on examination results within the state sector. The Chief Inspector of Schools in England immediately attacked this speech, saying "Heads in inner-city London, Birmingham, Manchester and Leeds haven't got the time to worry whether their children are climbing trees proficiently. These heads know that gaining academic qualifications is the one route out of poverty and disadvantage."[2] I can understand both of these perspectives. Of course, play and happiness are important, and I love to sit alongside my grandchildren as they play on the beach, climb trees and build imaginary worlds with whatever is at hand. But I agree with Sen when he says that 'aside from the recognition that happiness is valuable in itself, we must take note of the fact that the achievement of other things that we do value (and have reason to value) very often influences our sense of happiness – generated by that fulfillment'.[3] In other words, we cannot separate happiness from achievements and opportunities to achieve in life.

This book challenges the divide between the private and the state educational systems in the UK. Having attended a direct-grant school in the 1960s I came face-to-face with students who did not pay fees (because they had passed the 11+ examination) and those who did pay fees. My husband, Ian, was plucked from his working-class home in Hertfordshire when he won a scholarship to Rugby School in the 1950s. I have witnessed the privilege that this has given him. The direct-grant system that I experienced and the scholarship system that enabled my husband to attend an elite private school were only available for a select few. I argue in this book that such selective systems are no longer an option. I welcome recent discussions about the need for private and state school heads to join forces in order to build a fairer society. I hope that within my lifetime the stark divide in educational opportunities for young people in England will be eroded. But I do not believe that this will happen in a city such as Bristol unless heads of state and private schools work together, taking a shared responsibility for the education of all young people in order to build a stronger and more just society.

Rosamund Sutherland
Bristol, October 2013

Notes

[1] The Headmasters' and Headmistresses' Conference, the organisation that represents the elite private schools in the UK.

[2] www.bbc.co.uk/news/education-24367150.

[3] Sen, 2008, p 26.

CHAPTER ONE

An unfolding story

Introduction

This book has been inspired by my desire to write about the persistent and pervasive injustices within the English education system, injustices that I believe are as severe today as they were when I was a young girl in the 1950s. In writing this book, I aim to challenge current policy and practice by presenting a coherent argument about the ways in which the school system could change in order to address issues of education and social justice. I aim to question the dominant role of high-stakes assessment in education. I want to understand why schools have not embraced the transformative potential of digital technologies. And I want to move beyond the current polarised debate about the role of knowledge and skills within the curriculum.

Throughout the book, I draw on my research on the role of digital technologies in learning, research on mathematics education and research on the professional development of teachers. I also weave in reflections of my own education, and the educational history of my family, because this has influenced my views about the role of schools and education in society. At the same time, the book is influenced and underpinned by theoretical perspectives that enable me to interrogate issues that are relevant to the topic of education and social justice in a digital age.

The book has been written at a time of huge educational policy changes in England, changes to the curriculum, changes to assessment and changes to teacher education, and my questioning of these changes has influenced the writing of this book. In many respects, the book has become a case study of the school system in England, a study that also raises issues that are both more general and more global than is the case for one country.

This first chapter sets the scene for the whole book by emphasising the inequalities in educational opportunities that exist for young people in England. I introduce the debate about the future of schooling in the 21st century in order to reveal and challenge the dominant thinking about the ways in which digital technologies will change education. The chapter ends by presenting an overview of the whole book.

Before this, however, I start with reflections on the educational history of myself and my family in order to emphasise both the differential nature of educational opportunities and the potential of education to open up opportunities, to influence what young people are able to be and to become.

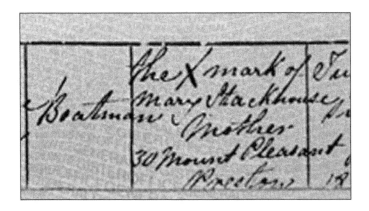

A personal history

Some years ago, when delving into my father's family history, I was confronted with the mark that my great-great-grandmother made on the birth certificate of her son, a mark that signified that she could not write her name, a mark that signified that she was illiterate. And it was the same for my mother's great-grandmother. It was a surprise to discover that women in my family of only three generations ago were illiterate. Why did this shock me? I was born just after the Second World War, and my own parents had been the first generation in their family to go to university. I was brought up to believe that education was a human right and university was a possibility. Writing was something learned when I first went to school, something I took for granted. Exploring my family history made me realise that my great-great-grandparents did not go to school. They were born in the 1840s, just before the Industrial Revolution and before the Elementary Education Act of 1870, which introduced universal education into England. Whereas schools existed before 1870, they were mainly for the wealthy and attendance was not compulsory.

My own early schooling in the 1950s was at a primary school in South Wales and the brand-new school symbolised a confidence and belief in the education of the children from the old and new town of Cwmbran. I had recently moved to this new town because my father

2

had taken up a job as a research physicist in the newly built factory of British Nylon Spinners.[1] This factory was to produce the nylon that offered to release women from the drudgery of ironing, the fabric that was embraced by Mary Quant in the 1960s when she designed the now-ubiquitous nylon tights, enabling her to create 'an integrated design aesthetic which made 1960s femininity suddenly synonymous with movement and energy'.[2] Towards the end of my primary schooling,

I moved to a small village school in Raglan and began to realise that only one or two in my class would pass the 11+ examination that opened up a grammar school education. I felt the brutality of a system that was to provide me with an academic education while almost all my classmates were offered a place in a secondary modern school.[3]

I knew that only a small proportion of my generation would go to university and that I would have to do well in my Ordinary (O) and Advanced (A) level examinations[4] if I were to stand a chance of obtaining a university place. I was always told how exceptional it had been for my mother to have won a state scholarship to Queen Mary College London from her poor Norfolk family, living in a one-up-one-down house that still had no running water when we visited my grandfather in the 1960s. However, despite my own success, I was never comfortable with the fact that all but two of my class of primary school children were educated at a secondary modern school, leaving school before 16 with probably no qualifications of value. And when I became an Open University tutor in the late 1970s, I welcomed the opportunity to become a member of an institution that enabled higher education to become accessible to everyone, whatever their previous education and qualifications. By then, a comprehensive school system had replaced the divided educational system that I had experienced, and in the 1980s, my own children attended very good comprehensive schools in Hertfordshire. By the 1990s, the university system in the UK began to open up so that nowadays approximately 50% of young people progress to university, compared with 4% in the early 1960s.

However, access to university by social class has remained about the same, with a slight increase in the proportion of working-class students progressing to university at the beginning of the 21st century.[5] This proportion is projected to decrease with the introduction of high university tuition fees in England. More worryingly, a recent report found that independent fee-paying school pupils are over 22 times more likely to enter a highly selective university than state school children who are living in poverty, and 55 times more likely to gain a place at Oxford or Cambridge. The report concludes that the:

> stark university participation gaps are driven by significant gaps at GCSE level and before: independent school pupils were three and a half times more likely than Free School Meals (FSM) pupils to attain five GCSEs[6] with grades A★–C including English and maths.[7]

Many people argue that focusing attention on opportunities to attend university is elitist and that other forms of post-school progression are equally valuable. While not disagreeing with this view, I also believe that from a social justice perspective, all young people should be given the opportunity to gain the necessary qualifications to obtain a place at university. They can then choose whether they progress to university, other forms of further education, an apprenticeship or employment. I am sure that many of my old primary school classmates from the village of Raglan are nowadays enjoying their grandchildren as I am doing, but what is wrong is that without academic qualifications, they would have had more limited choices in terms of further education and more limited job opportunities than I had in the late 1960s.

My early research in the 1980s took me to challenging schools in London and I was always pushing the boundaries of what young people could learn, showing that with new teaching approaches and harnessing the power of new technologies, almost anything could be possible.[8] Whether in inner London schools or in schools in Mexico or Rwanda, my research has always been about what it is possible to learn and how computers could support students to learn that which was previously thought to be impossible. For example, Logo programming could enable complex mathematical ideas to become accessible to primary pupils,[9] and spreadsheets could be used to make algebra meaningful to vocational engineering students.[10] It now seems to me that it was naive to believe that digital technology on its own could play a role in democratising education and this issue is explored further throughout the book.

To conclude this opening section, I can now see that my research (which focused on the art of the possible), the educational experiences of my friends and family, and my general optimistic disposition meant that, for many years, I was more or less blind to the new educational divides that were opening up in the country. This began to change as I became involved in the rebuilding of a new school in South Bristol.

A developing divide

By the late 1990s, I was working as an academic at the University of Bristol and, by contrast to what I had experienced in Hertfordshire, I learned that many people were choosing to send their children to the numerous private and fee-charging schools in the city.[11] At this time, Bristol state schools were almost at the bottom of the school league tables, and when I became head of the University of Bristol's Graduate School of Education in 2003, I was often challenged about why such a successful department was not more involved in working to raise educational standards in Bristol's schools. Despite the fact that we trained over 200 secondary teachers a year, with the vast majority of these choosing to teach in state-maintained schools, and despite the fact that much of our research involved partnerships with state primary and secondary schools, the general perception in the city was that Bristol University was the 'University on the hill', with very little involvement with the local community. In 2006, the university was approached to become a sponsor of a new academy to be built in South Bristol, one of the most socially deprived areas of the city and the country as a whole. Without any hesitation, the Vice Chancellor, Eric Thomas, agreed that the university should sponsor this academy, and so began my involvement with Merchants' Academy in South Bristol.

When visiting Withywood Community School, the predecessor school, I was shocked by the state of repair of the building. I was shocked by the realisation that 83% of students failed both GCSE mathematics and English. I could see how difficult it was for these young people to continue to post-16 education and that it was almost impossible for any of them to progress to higher education. The palpable poverty of many of the parents was also shocking to me, a poverty that I had not directly witnessed since I had been at primary school in South Wales in the 1950s. When I attended an end-of-year awards ceremony, I could not understand why the performance of the choir was so poor. Surely, I thought, a choir can learn to sing beautifully whatever the background of the students. For me, the singing of this choir has come to symbolise a lack of expectations of the students, whether in music, in sport or in more academic areas. Recently, Gay Elms primary school has become part of Merchants' Academy and, by contrast, the choir from this school sings so beautifully that it is being invited to perform across Bristol. This demonstrates what is possible when an experienced singing teacher believes that children can learn how to sing, has very high expectations of what they can produce and knows how to lead so that the children learn to sing together as one choir. The singing of Gay Elms Choir represents for me the importance of teaching and the power of collective and cooperative production.

Through my involvement with Merchants' Academy, I have learned about the appalling educational opportunities for young people in South Bristol and the existence of persistent areas of deprivation. For example, in a report published in 2007, it was shown that less than 5% of young people from the Withywood community attended university compared with almost 50% in the more prosperous areas of the city.[12] I am horrified by the contrast between the relatively privileged state comprehensive education of my own children and the education of very many young people in South Bristol. This is not a difference between state and private education systems, but a difference between state schools in areas that are mostly attended by students from working-class backgrounds and state schools that are mostly attended by students from middle-class backgrounds. The situation is even worse when we factor in the difference between the educational opportunities for those who attend private schools compared to those who attend state schools. When reading Andrew Adonis's book,[13] I can appreciate why he calls these 'low-performing' schools 'comprehensive secondary modern schools', although I have always been a strong advocate of comprehensive education.

I continue to be concerned by the contrast in educational opportunities available to young people in South Bristol and those living in North Bristol through my evaluation of a programme that aims to inspire young people to follow careers in science and engineering (The Future Brunels Programme).[14] Each year, the programme selects 12 young people between the ages of 11 and 12, chosen from two schools in the north of Bristol and two in the south of Bristol, and works with them over a period of five years. When we examined the baseline data for the young people who started the programme in 2011/12, we found stark differences between the educational opportunities of young people from the south and the north of the city. The young people from South Bristol schools are less likely to obtain good grades in GCSE mathematics and English and are less likely to have the opportunity to study academic A levels in comparison with the young people from

North Bristol schools. They are also very unlikely to have members of their family who have studied at university, and unlikely to know anyone in their neighbourhood who has attended university. Of the six state secondary schools in South Bristol, only three have sixth forms, with two of these opening recently and not yet having a track record of students passing A level examinations and progressing to university. By contrast, in North Bristol, all the state secondary schools either offer A level courses or are affiliated to a thriving sixth form college with a very good track record of students gaining places at university. This represents a manifestly severe injustice,[15] an injustice in both educational opportunities and related life chances.

I have used the example of Bristol to highlight issues that are replicated across the country.[16] I question how people in a city such as Bristol and other similar cities have let a situation of 'severe injustice' continue into the 21st century. I wonder if the new elected Mayor of Bristol will try to tackle this issue. Why does no one appear to take a top-down perspective and ask what can be done immediately for young people in South Bristol? This is a collective challenge for South Bristol (and for other similar communities) and cannot be solved by schools taking isolated perspectives. It is important that the governors of Merchants' Academy appreciate that a flourishing sixth form offering both academic and vocational opportunities is an issue of social justice for all the young people who live in South Bristol, and not just for students who attend this particular school. How could a system that had supported my father and mother to be educated and attend university from working-class families in the 1930s not be supporting young people nowadays from similar backgrounds?

In many respects, politicians recognised this 'severe injustice' when they set up the Academy programme at the beginning of the 21st century. Although not without criticism,[17] the key objective of the new Academies was to replace 'failing' schools with 'successful all-ability schools, founded and managed on a different and better basis'.[18] They were also intended to overcome the destructive division between state and private schools and the 'absence of sixth forms in the half of the country – mostly the deprived half – where comprehensives stopped education at the age of sixteen'.[19]

At a similar time that the Academy programme was being used to change the education system in England, the Building Schools of the Future (BSF) programme[20] was set up in order to invest in new school buildings in England. However, it is interesting that many of the aims of the BSF programme seem to have been at odds with the aims of the Academy programme, and, in particular, the vision of how digital technologies should change 21st-century education. Although Adonis, the chief architect of the Academies programme, acknowledges that he harnessed the BSF programme in order to expand the Academy programme, he hardly mentions the role of digital technologies in his book *Education, education, education*.[21] It seems as if policymakers either wholeheartedly embrace the digital and argue for the end of schooling as we know it (as in the BSF programme), or ignore the digital and focus on improving the performance of schools (as in the Academies programme). But, as I shall argue in Chapter Two, digital technologies are now part of the fabric of our lives and so somehow have to be integrated into the life of schools. However, my view on how this should happen differs from the dominant view about how digital technologies will impact on schools and education, as I begin to explain in the next section of this chapter.

A digital revolution?

> Just as the industrial revolution transformed the home and created the school in order to provide a disciplined workforce for the new factories and offices, the digital and communications revolution seems likely to transform the learning environment for today's young people. In tandem with this, rapidly accelerating change in other areas – in economics, in demographics, in our social and cultural life, in government policy, in the management of education and in developments in pedagogy – will also play a key role in the shape of future learning.[22]

The debate about the future of schooling dominated the first decade of the 21st century, and the BSF programme in England was viewed as an opportunity to create a new vision for schooling and education. Many people argue that the rapid development of Information and Communications Technology (ICT) and its integration into school life offers the potential for new models of learning to emerge in schools, less restricted by the infrastructure and hierarchy of the traditional classroom. The idea of flexible and what are sometimes called 21st-century learning skills (eg critical thinking, problem-solving, communicating) permeated the thinking behind the BSF programme, with the claim being made that such skills are important in preparing young people for the 21st-century world of work. The local authorities that were awarded BSF funding developed their own vision documents, which often explicitly addressed the issue of education and deprivation. For example:

> Education is at the heart of Birmingham's renaissance and is fundamental to supporting the Community Strategy. The transformed education system envisaged in the Education Vision will break the current cycle of deprivation and poverty. It will do this by raising the attainment and achievement of all Birmingham's young citizens and equipping them with flexible qualities and skills that lead both to employment and economic prosperity in the 21st Century.[23]

Many people have been questioning the role of schooling in the 21st century, and this questioning is always linked to young people's participation in digital cultures. The boundaries between formal education and informal learning are considered to be breaking down, as are the barriers to online learning.[24] Whereas some people argue that schools will continue to have a role in society within the 21st century, there are others who suggest that schools are outdated and anachronistic organisations, and that, in the future, traditional classrooms will become redundant.

> Home-based study using computers will probably result in part-time attendance at school. As young people spend more and more time surfing the net, accessing virtual libraries, conferencing with their teachers via the web and publishing their work electronically, the traditional classroom as a setting for learning is quickly becoming redundant.[25]

However, there is an alternative perspective that I shall return to in future chapters. This alternative perspective argues that it is knowledge and not skills that should be at the core of an education system, and that from a knowledge perspective, the boundaries between school and out-of-school need to be maintained. Interestingly, schools that have been built as part of the BSF programme do not look that different from schools that were built in the 1950s and this, I suggest, is because there is something timeless about schools as institutions that bring together young people to learn and create new knowledge that enables them to flourish as human beings, as well as preparing them for participation in society.

This book

This book consists of eight chapters, each one of them addressing different aspects of the arguments and narratives that make up the whole. Chapter One has introduced two themes that set the scene for the book. The first is concerned with the divide in terms of educational opportunities available to young people in England today. The second raises questions about the ways in which the digital landscape changes the nature of the debate about equity and social justice in education.

Chapter Two draws on sociocultural theory in order to argue that human action is mediated by social, institutional and cultural factors, which include the technologies that have been invented by humans in order to transform our abilities to achieve and perform. I argue that if digital technologies are available resources, then it is important that young people learn how to convert these resources into what Sen calls capabilities,[26] that is, opportunities that can be realised in action. I argue that one of the roles of schools is to teach young people to convert digital resources into capabilities and that currently teachers are constrained from doing this by the school system.

Chapter Three argues that a curriculum for a just society has to recognise the competing ideologies in the 21st-century curriculum, which centre around a tension between knowledge and skills. I suggest that there is a divide with respect to the curriculum being offered in schools, and that this divide tends to be patterned along social class lines. Schools that serve predominantly working-class communities are more likely to have adopted a skills-based curriculum, with an emphasis on vocational courses, whereas schools that serve more middle-class communities are more likely to offer a knowledge-based curriculum, with an emphasis on academic courses.

Chapter Four discusses Vygotsky's distinction between everyday and academic knowledge in order to argue that one of the purposes of schooling is to introduce young people to bodies of 'academic' knowledge that they are not likely to bump into out of school. I argue that academic knowledge does not emerge spontaneously from everyday knowledge and so celebrating everyday knowledge can become a barrier to learning academic knowledge. I also suggest that it is important to understand the tension between everyday and academic knowledge within a digital age, because out-of-school uses of digital technologies can get in the way of what a teacher is intending to teach. This perspective contrasts with a dominant view that young people's use of digital technologies should lead to an erosion of the boundaries between home and school.

Chapter Five looks more closely at schools as institutions and their intellectual, visual and material impact on society. I contrast the school buildings of the elite private schools with the buildings of state schools and suggest that the recent rebuilding of secondary schools in England has been positive in terms of valuing the education of young people within disadvantaged communities. I discuss Olson's distinction between personally held beliefs and Knowledge with a capital K, a distinction that is similar to Vygotsky's distinction between everyday and academic knowledge, and use this distinction to criticise the recent emphasis on personalised learning and the way in which this becomes intertwined with ideas about education in a digital age.

Chapter Six focuses on the tension between the use of school league tables to identify the differences between schools in terms of educational opportunities available to young people and the unintended consequences of high-stakes performance measures. I argue for radical changes to the assessment system so that teachers can focus on teaching for engagement with knowledge, as opposed to 'teaching to the test'. I suggest that the most important form of assessment is feedback on students' learning and that such feedback can be used to challenge low expectations of students. Suggestions are also made for assessment systems that harness the potential of digital technologies as tools for constructing knowledge and developing the capabilities for actively participating in society.

Chapter Seven starts by re-emphasising my view that the purpose of education is to develop the capabilities that enable young people to both flourish as human beings and participate in society, and that this includes learning 'powerful knowledge'. I argue that such powerful knowledge is organised around coherent, connected and complex collections of concepts, and, in this respect, is different from the everyday knowledge that people learn out of school. The chapter continues by emphasising the importance of teachers and teaching, focusing on the role of knowledge-building in the classroom, including a discussion of the ways in which human activity is mediated by knowledge objects.

Chapter Eight reconsiders the main arguments made throughout the book, and starts by revisiting the idea of capabilities, discussing what practical actions could be taken in order to address issues of social injustice. The importance of cooperation between schools and between students within schools is discussed. The chapter then considers professional development as a process of innovation, highlighting the role of leadership and the importance of collaboration and cooperation between schools. Finally, the chapter ends with a personal reflection on the pleasures of finishing a piece of work, and the pleasure of creative production.

Through the process of writing, I have challenged my own views and the views of others, and revealed contradictions in my own thinking. Through writing the book, I am clearer about the need for the educational system in England to urgently address the manifest injustices that exist within the system, injustices that result in whole communities of young people having severely restricted life chances. Of course, I know that education cannot address all of the injustices in society, but writing this book has made me more convinced that schools can make a difference.

Notes

[1.] British Nylon Spinners opened in 1948, and, at the time, boasted the largest factory floor in Europe. It ceased operating in 1988.

[2.] Taken from Angela Robbie's oration for Mary Quant. Available at: http://diyiyeok01.eblog.cz/oration-for-mary-quant-363.html#respond

[3.] The 11+ examination was created by the Butler Education Act 1944, which aimed to create a tripartite system of education, with an academic, a technical and a vocational strand. The 11+ examination was taken by children at the end of primary school, and only those who passed this examination were able to progress to the academic strand of education (approximately 25%). Those children who failed the 11+ examination were sent to secondary modern schools.

[4.] O and A level examinations were introduced in the 1950s for those students who were following an academic education. O level examinations were usually taken at 16+ and A level examinations at 18+. These qualifications were replaced in 1988 by the General Certificate of Secondary Education (GCSE). Since 2004, secondary schools in England have been judged by how many of their students pass at least five GCSEs, including English and mathematics, and these results are published in league tables.

[5.] Vignoles et al (2004).

[6.] The GCSE is a qualification taken in a number of subjects at 16+.

[7.] Sutton Trust (2010).

[8.] Hoyle and Sutherland (1989); Sutherland (1989, 1992)

[9.] See, for example, Hoyles and Noss (1992).

[10.] See, for example, Sutherland et al (1996).

[11.] The city of Bristol 'has the highest concentration of independent school places outside of a small exclusive corner of north London that includes Hampstead and Highgate, and some of the poorest-performing state schools. It is one of only a handful of areas outside the south-east where independent schools outnumber secondary schools, with a private-school tradition stretching back 500 years'. See www.guardian.co.uk/education/2008/jan/29/publicschools.schools

[12.] Raphael Reed et al (2007).

[13.] Adonis (2012). See also Sutton trust (2011).

[14.] The Future Brunels Programme is run by Rhian Tritton and Rachel Roberts. See www.ssgreatbritain.org/about-us/press/introducing-trust's-12-new-'future-brunels' and Eagle and Sutherland (2012).

[15.] Sen (2009, p 21).

[16.] For further discussion of this issue, see Marshall (2013).

[17.] See, for example, Benn (2011).

[18.] Adonis (2012, p 323).

[19.] Adonis (2012, p 326).

[20.] National Audit Office (2009).

[21.] Adonis (2012).

[22.] 21st Century Schools (2004, p 10).

[23.] Birmingham (2009, p 4).

[24.] Facer (2011).

[25.] 21st Century Schools (2004).

[26.] Sen (2001).

CHAPTER TWO

Expanding the possible: people and technologies

Introducing the digital

I first met a computer when I began to learn computer programming as an undergraduate in 1967, and then worked as a programmer for several years after graduating from university. The change from the huge mainframe machine to my beautiful portable computer could not have been imagined in the 1960s. And I am convinced that using a computer has transformed what I can do, transformed my abilities. In the late 1980s, I bought my first portable computer and since then, all my academic work has been produced with a portable machine, working at the kitchen table, working as I travel. I love writing, but with shaky spelling and appalling handwriting, I very much doubt that

I could have become an academic if constrained to writing with pen and paper. I struggle to organise physical paperwork, but in a digital environment, can always search for and find the necessary documents. I can work collaboratively with colleagues at a distance through electronic communication and work with students in faraway countries such as Botswana, Rwanda, Chile and Mexico. I can download an electronic book onto my iPad, and access journals immediately. I can play around with unknown quantities in a spreadsheet in order to plan a budget. The technology constantly changes and nowadays computers can be used as much for leisure as for work. For example, I use digital devices to watch replays of television programmes, to navigate on a boat and to find recipes that fit the ingredients at hand.

I was an Open University tutor in the 1970s, before electronic communication was available, and, at that time, I used the telephone for one-to-one tutorials and the postal system to give written feedback to students. As humans, we are adept at using whatever technology is at hand and as new technologies develop, we learn to exploit them in our day-to-day lives. For me, the advantages of hand-held technologies with instant connectivity outweigh the disadvantages. They enable me to look after my grandchildren while also keeping in touch with work. Digital technologies have become part of the fabric of our lives and we can choose what we appropriate and what we reject. I am resisting using Facebook and Twitter, although this may have changed by the time this book is published. I have only recently started to read ebooks and still very much prefer the physicality of a paper book. I can sometimes believe that the old way is better than the digital innovation, for example, in my use of a paper-and-pencil diary. And nowadays, with instant connectivity, it is possible to waste time browsing the Internet when I should be focusing on academic work. But, overall, I am convinced that my career as an academic has been inextricably linked to the potential that the computer and digital technologies have offered me and is also, in some ways, linked to the history of the development of the personal computer.

This is a personal story of how I have used digital technologies to empower and liberate myself. All of us who exploit this power will have different stories to tell, which relate to our day-to-day lives and work. But the story of how I have embraced the digital could go hand-in-hand with the story of how I continue to value non-digital technologies, using a paper diary, doing rough calculations on the back of an envelope, reading picture books to my grandchildren, shopping in a market and travelling to meet people face to face.

My first research project as an academic was concerned with how Logo programming could be used to support the learning of mathematics.[1] This and subsequent research has shown how digital technologies can be used to transform learning in schools.[2] But while there is extensive evidence of what is possible, schools and teachers are not embracing the potential that had been imagined in the 1980s.

This chapter starts by emphasising that we live in a world that is full of invented technologies and that as humans, we creatively adapt these 'things' in our day-to-day lives. Invented technologies can be digital (eg a mobile phone) or non-digital (eg a paper book). This chapter, then, presents a brief history of digital technologies and schooling, tracing the time from when the Logo programming language was first introduced into schools to the present time, when, interestingly, there is a renewed interest in computer programming. The chapter then briefly examines how institutional structures constrain the ways in which teachers adopt digital technologies in classroom practices. It then draws on sociocultural theory to discuss the ways in which technologies, in particular, digital technologies, can be used to transform learning and expand what it is possible for humans to achieve. Finally, the chapter introduces Sen's theory of capabilities, and argues that from a social justice perspective, schools should be introducing young people to the transformative potential of digital technologies.

People and designed objects

> The environments in which humans live are thick with invented artefacts that are in constant use for structuring activity, for saving mental work, or for avoiding errors or they are adapted creatively almost without notice. These ubiquitous mediating structures that both organise and constrain activity include not only designed objects such as tools, control instruments, and symbolic representations like graphs, diagrams, text, plans and pictures, but people in social relations, as well as features and landmarks in the physical environment.[3]

I have used this quote, written by Roy Pea in 1993, for many years in my writing and teaching. The quote represents what I believe is important about people and technology. Pea emphasises the fact that the environments in which humans live are full of 'invented artefacts'. And what is crucial here is the idea of humans inventing 'things' that potentially transform the ways in which we interact with the world. When my great-grandparents were alive, they would have journeyed by foot or by horse and this limited their mobility and their work possibilities. By the end of the 19th century, the bicycle had become an available form of transport, and this invention, which enabled people to

move almost four times as fast as they could walk, allowed people to travel further to their place of work and made it possible for those who lived in a city to travel into the countryside for leisure. The bicycle also had a huge impact on the emancipation of women and influenced female fashion of the time.[4]

The example of the invention of the bicycle draws attention to the ways in which technology potentially changes our lives. But it seems to be easier for us to understand how 'invented things' change physical interactions than it is to understand how they change mental interactions with the world. Physical interactions can be seen, whereas mental interactions are mostly invisible. Also, within the West, we live in a culture that values the individual, autonomy and personal achievement.[5] In focusing on the individual, we tend not to focus on the ways in which individual achievements are supported by both people and technology. We celebrate the idea of the 'lone scientist' interacting with the world, and do not pay attention to the fact that individual activity is always situated within a social and cultural context.

Within the earlier quotation, Pea says that invented things are used to structure activity and save mental work, and it is this idea that I believe is important from a social justice perspective. I personally have exploited the potential of a word processor to structure my writing, to transform my ability to organise paperwork and to help to get into the flow of writing. There are many examples of 'invented technologies' that potentially transform our ability to do something. For example, the long division algorithm written on paper with a pen or a pencil and brought into common use in the 16th century enables us to carry out computations that would be very difficult or impossible to do mentally. The use of a watch, invented in the 17th century, enables us to both monitor and synchronise time. The use of a dictionary expands our vocabulary and understanding of the meaning of words, and the metal filing cabinet, invented at the beginning of the 19th century, potentially transforms the way we structure and organise paperwork.[6]

Pea goes on to say that as humans, we creatively adapt whatever has been designed for our own purposes, which could be far from the designer's intentions. For example, a watch can be adapted to become a navigation tool, a ruler can be used to cut paper and a piece of paper can be turned into a paper aeroplane. Technology can also be creatively adapted for educational purposes that were not intended by the designers, as when spreadsheets are used to support students to learn algebra.[7]

Pea also emphasises that designed objects both organise and constrain. There is some pressure at work for me to use a digital calendar, but I choose not to use one because I have found that it constrains my thinking about time. I prefer to scribble a future event, such as 'going on holiday', into a paper diary without specifying a time, and I find that digital diaries constrain me to enter an event into a time slot. I like the physical tangible presence of paper books and enjoy looking at my bookshelf at work and choosing a book to share with a colleague. This is not possible with e-books, where there is nothing tangible to pass on. I like writing in the margins of physical books, and do not find it so pleasurable to do this when I am reading a digital book. I find that a digital book constrains me to read in a linear way, and does not allow me to flick back and forwards between different chapters.

Digital environments tend to require precision and do not readily accommodate the rough sketch. My architect daughter, for example, is always sketching on paper as well as designing in a 3D digital environment because the paper-and-pencil sketch allows her to create in a non-linear way, allows her to roughly experiment with design ideas and allows her to communicate new ideas to a client. Sennett, in his book *The craftsman*, suggests that 'the tactile, the relational and the incomplete are physical experiences that occur in the act of drawing'.[8] By contrast,

he argues that what appears on the screen of computer-aided design (CAD) packages is 'impossibly coherent, framed in a unified way that the physical sight never is'.[9]

The point I want to emphasise here is that we can make choices about the technologies we choose to use, whether digital or non-digital, and it is important to ask questions about the ways in which a particular technology can be used to potentially transform our abilities, and interactions with the world.[10] For example, what does collaborative writing with Google Scholar offer that is different from a word-processed document shared by email? What is the difference between an online meeting and a meeting face to face? What is the difference between following a paper-based recipe for baking a cake and watching a Youtube video?

In focusing attention on designed objects, it is important not to lose sight of the fact that humans are situated in social and cultural practices and that participation in these practices provides the fundamental mechanism for learning and knowing. What Pea, in the earlier quote, calls 'people in social relations' tends to be underemphasised in much of the discussion about the transformative potential of digital technologies and often seems to be ignored by those who design digital technologies. For example, designers of technology for pre-school children often produce environments for very young children to interact with on their own, although we know that young children learn from talking and participating with their parents and other adults.[11] I use the example of very young children because this draws attention to the ways in which software designers can ignore the social aspects of learning. There are many ways in which our interactions with people structure and support what we learn, whether we learn by participating alongside an expert (eg when an apprentice surgeon begins to assist in operations), whether we learn by an adult doing some of the work for us (eg when a parent does some of the jigsaw for a toddler), whether we learn from peer group interaction, or whether we learn from explicit teaching. In all of these situations, 'more knowledgeable others' are crucial and critical and it is now widely recognised that humans are the only species in which parents teach their young, the only species that expects to learn from others.[12]

A brief history of digital technologies and education

Invented technologies were used in schools before the digital age, for example, the globe in geography, log tables in mathematics, the recorder in music, the atomic table in chemistry and the tape recorder in modern foreign languages. Some technologies were designed for individual use (eg the slate board) and others were designed for the teacher to communicate to the class (eg the blackboard). Some technologies are used in the practices of experts outside school (the atomic table, the set square, the piano) and others have been designed primarily for educational purposes (eg the textbook, the digital floor turtle). Some technologies drop out of use (eg the slide rule) because they are replaced by newer technologies (the calculator), and other technologies continue to be used (eg the pencil), even when they could be replaced by newer digital technologies.

The computer and digital technologies began to be introduced into schools in the 1980s. In 1980, Seymour Papert wrote:

> Our culture is so mathphobic, so math-fearing that if I could demonstrate how the computer can bring us into a new relationship to mathematics, I would have a strong foundation for claiming that the computer has the ability to change our relationship to other kinds of learning we might fear.[13]

My early research on Logo programming was influenced by this view, and, at the time, we believed that the use of computers could and would radically change the teaching and learning of mathematics. Working in inner London schools in the late 1980s, we spent three years carrying out a longitudinal study of what secondary students could learn about mathematics through Logo programming.

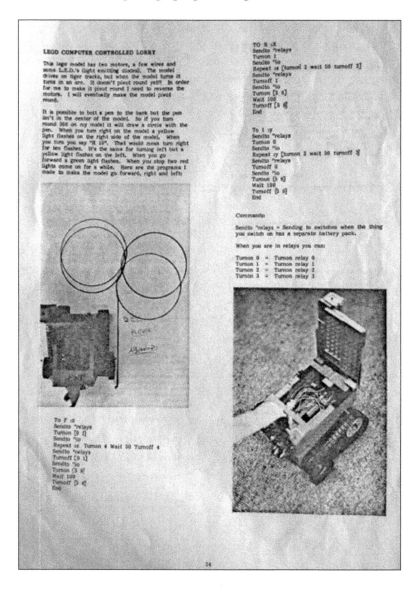

At a similar time, my son was learning Logo at his primary school as part of the Chiltern Logo Project.[14] He built a robot in Lego and programmed it to draw using sensors. The idea that primary school pupils could program in Logo seemed revolutionary at the time because computer programming was viewed as being a practice of adults and the mathematically related ideas of programming, such as variable and recursion, were considered to be too difficult for primary-aged pupils.

By the late 1980s, teachers were beginning to experiment with using computers and standalone software within a range of subjects, for example, the use of data-logging in science, the use of multimedia in English and history, and the use of dynamic geometry within mathematics, and the English National Curriculum began to specify particular uses of computers within a range of subjects. By the late 1990s, schools in England were beginning to get Internet access and new visions for how technology might change education were emerging. What was originally called IT (Information Technology) was now called ICT, incorporating the letter C for the word Communication. The focus on the use of computers across the curriculum began to shift to a focus on how the Internet could be used as a means of accessing information, and as a means of communication. A view began to emerge that with access to the Internet, young people would be able to learn 'anywhere' and 'anytime', and that boundaries between out-of-school and in-school learning would blur (I discuss in the next chapter why I think this view is misconceived). Research on young people's use of digital technologies outside school showed that they were engaging with digital technologies for both educational and leisure purposes[15] and such findings began to play into a debate about the future of schooling.

At the end of the 20th century, the term 'Web 2.0' was coined to refer to new forms of open-source applications that facilitate collaboration and information-sharing (eg wikis, blogs, social bookmarking). Digital technology develops rapidly and, as with previous developments (eg standalone software, the Internet), the advent of Web 2.0 technologies led to new visions about how such technologies would change education and schooling. Alongside such developments, some people predicted the demise of schools and the rise of a more individualised provision of education.[16]

At the time of writing, the latest wave of technology innovation relates to the use of the Cloud for storing data, alongside the use of mobile technologies and application software for mobile devices (called apps). As with the other waves of technology innovation, some schools and teachers are enthusiastically embracing the potential of portable tablets, believing that the mere introduction of the technology into schools will change practices of teaching and enhance student learning. However, I suggest that unless such innovations are accompanied by sustained professional development and a process of evaluation, there will be minimal long-term effects. Believing that the technology alone will somehow 'cause' the desired changes is one of the biggest barriers to productive uses of digital technologies for teaching and learning.

Alongside the use of ICT across the curriculum, ICT became a curriculum subject in 1989 and there is often a tension within schools about what should be taught in ICT lessons and how ICT should be used within other curriculum subjects. The following is an example of what the majority of primary pupils were expected to have learned within the ICT curriculum by the end of primary school:

> Pupils understand the need for care in framing questions when collecting, finding and interrogating information. They interpret their findings, question plausibility and recognise that poor-quality information leads to unreliable results. They add to, amend and combine different forms of information from a variety of sources. They use ICT to present information in different forms and show they are aware of the intended audience and the need for quality in their presentations. They exchange information and ideas with others in a variety of ways, including using e-mail. They use ICT systems to control events in a predetermined manner and to sense physical data. They use ICT-based models and simulations to explore patterns and relationships, and make predictions about the consequences of their decisions. They compare their use of ICT with other methods and with its use outside school. (Level 4 ICT curriculum)[17]

There are elements of this 'attainment target' that refer to critically engaging with information accessed from the Internet, elements that refer to using sensors within control technology and elements that relate to the use of ICT within mathematics and statistics. In this sense, there is a tension between what might be taught within other curriculum areas and what should be taught within the ICT curriculum. The breadth of scope also raises questions about how ICT teachers could have adequate expertise across all of these subject areas. In trying to do all of these things, ICT in schools often ends up by not engaging deeply with any of these substantive areas and in 2011, the chairman of Google said that the country that had invented the computer was 'throwing away your great computer heritage by failing to teach computing in schools'.[18] At a similar time the report 'Computing in schools: shut down or restart' was published by the Royal Society,[19] and it claimed that:

Although existing curricula for Information and Communication Technology (ICT) are broad and allow scope for teachers to inspire pupils and help them develop interests in Computing, many pupils are not inspired by what they are taught and gain nothing beyond basic digital literacy skills such as how to use a word-processor or a database.[20]

The report recommended that the term 'ICT' should no longer be used and the associated concept should be disaggregated into digital literacy, information technology and computer science. Overall, the report called for a re-emphasis of computer science and computer programming (such as Scratch,[21] educational microcontroller kits such as Arduino and robot kits such as Lego Mindstorms).

By the beginning of 2012, and clearly influenced by this report, the Coalition government announced that ICT would be replaced by 'rigorous computer science':

Imagine the dramatic change which could be possible in just a few years, once we remove the roadblock of the existing ICT curriculum. Instead of children bored out of their minds being taught how to use Word and Excel by bored teachers, we could have 11-year-olds able to write simple 2D computer animations using an MIT [Massachusetts Institute of Technology] tool called Scratch. By 16, they could have an understanding of formal logic previously covered only in University courses and be writing their own Apps for smartphones.[22]

So, almost 30 years after Logo programming was first introduced into schools, and after many years in which its potential has been ignored, computer programming appears to be coming back in again. Whereas I welcome this move in many respects, it also indicates that policymakers are not recognising the complex ways in which the digital is integrated into the fabric of our lives, and what this could mean for how digital technologies could be integrated into the fabric of schools.

Jenkins argues for the importance of what he calls media literacy skills, which enable people to participate in society.[23] This includes such skills as the ability to interact with tools that expand mental capacities (as discussed earlier), the ability to pool knowledge and compare notes with others towards a common goal, and the ability to evaluate the reliability and credibility of different information sources. Jenkins also argues that young people have unequal access to such digital literacies (a participation gap) and that there should be a paradigm shift within schools in terms of how each subject (eg history, mathematics) is taught. He argues that media literacy should not be an add-on subject, but should permeate all school subjects. He also argues that there should be a shift in the focus of literacy from individual expression to community involvement: 'The new literacies almost all involve social skills, developed through collaboration and networking. These skills build on the foundation of traditional literacy and research, technical, and critical-analysis skills learned in the classroom'.[24] Such community involvement is reflected in the rise of what are called hackerspaces, where like-minded people come together to collaborate, share ideas and make technology-enabled products. In some ways, this maker subculture is a technology-based development of do-it-yourself culture.

> Typical interests enjoyed by the maker subculture include engineering-oriented pursuits such as electronics, robotics, 3-D printing, and the use of CNC [computer numerically controlled] tools, as well as more traditional activities such as metalworking, woodworking, and traditional arts and crafts. The subculture stresses new and unique applications of technologies, and encourages invention and prototyping. There is a strong focus on using and learning practical skills and applying them creatively.[25]

Institutional factors that influence how digital technologies are used in schools

Within my early research, I was involved in what I call bottom-up research and development projects, working with teachers on the ground, and I believed that this was the way to bring about change in classrooms. However, I began to understand that there are limitations to such a bottom-up approach, and in 2005, within the InterActive Education project, we started to take a more holistic perspective, both examining learning at the level of the classroom and taking into account the institutional and societal factors that structure learning.[26] Taking such a perspective, we came to understand the challenges that teachers face when considering using digital technologies in the classroom. For example, at that time, we found that the mandate for ICT in education (in England) had overwhelmingly been interpreted by schools as a licence to acquire equipment. Such a focus on the acquisition of equipment emphasised the technology and not the people using the technology. Furthermore, we found evidence of teachers devolving their responsibility for teaching to the technology itself, thinking that the mere use of ICT would lead to changes in learning. Such a focus on acquiring equipment also detracted from an emphasis on the professional development that teachers need in order to change established practices.

When we examine the societal and institutional factors that structure the use of ICT in schools, we can begin to appreciate why teachers might not be embracing digital technologies for teaching and learning. For example, in England many schools have recently invested in Virtual Learning Environments (VLEs) and this widespread adoption of VLEs seems to be getting in the way of bottom-up innovation at the level of the classroom:

> far from being a source of enabling 'bottom-up' change, these institutional technologies appear to be entwined in a multiplicity of 'top-down' relationships related to the concerns of school management and administration. It could be argued that the use of these systems is shaped more often by concerns of institutional efficiency, modernisation and rationalisation, rather than the individual concerns of learners or teachers. Indeed despite the connotations of the 'Learning Platform' and 'virtual learning environment' it would seem that the primary concern of these technologies is – at best – with a limited bureaucratic 'vision of academic success' based around qualifications and grades (Pring, 2010, p. 84). With these issues in mind, we therefore need to approach institutional technologies in terms of enforcing the bureaucratic interests of the institution rather than expanding the educational interests of the individual.[27]

As Selwyn suggests, it is important to understand the policy and institutional context in which digital technologies are being introduced into schools. Without such an understanding, we may attribute lack of change in classrooms to, for example, lack of training of teachers, or to teachers' resistance to change, whereas there may be more complex and interrelated factors that need to be understood if we are going to be able to use ICT to innovate at the level of the classroom.

In a recent project, I have been working with schools that were funded through the Building Schools of the Future programme to support teachers to use digital technologies to change practices of teaching and learning. We are finding that the schools still seem to expect that the technology on its own will almost 'magically' do the work for them. For example, one of the schools was persuaded by a commercial company that their software would provide dashboard systems for individual assessment of students. Another school believed that a class set of kindles would help reluctant readers to learn to read. Another school believed that their VLE would somehow transform teaching and learning. In none of these cases was there any critical thinking about how such 'technology solutions' would work, no thinking through of the ways in which people together with these technologies might be able to change practices, and no thinking about how to evaluate the innovations with technology with respect to the aims of the innovation. Without such thinking and a willingness to learn from experimentation and existing research evidence, there is likely to be very little impact of digital technologies on teaching and learning in any of these schools. I return to this issue when discussing innovation and professional development in Chapter Seven.

We are finding that whereas schools are investing huge amounts of money on VLEs, many teachers appear to be resistant to using the centralised systems produced by commercial companies. However, at the same time, there seems to be a bottom-up interest in the use of freely available social learning platforms, for example, Edmodo.[28] As with Facebook, Edmodo is free to use, and adoption seems to be taking place at a grassroots level, rather than senior management mandating its use. A teacher recently explained to me that he thought that Edmodo has potential because students find it easy to use and they can communicate online. As a mathematics teacher, he is finding that he can use Edomodo to support students to work collaboratively online when solving mathematical problems for homework.

Transforming learning: expanding the possible

While writing this chapter, I have lived through the 2012 Olympics and Paralympics and witnessed the way in which an athlete's body can be transformed by technology. In watching the Paralympics, the audience focused on what athletes could achieve and not on their particular abilities and disabilities. The Paralympics have raised the issue about whether the use of an 'assistive technology' can enable a 'disabled' athlete to perform better than an 'able-bodied' athlete:

> How could someone without lower legs possibly have an advantage over athletes with natural legs? The debate took a scientific turn in 2007 when a German team reported that

Pistorius used 25 percent less energy than natural runners. The conclusion was tied to the unusual prosthetic device made by an Icelandic company called Össur. The Flex-Foot Cheetah has become the go-to running prosthetic for Paralympic (and, potentially Olympic) athletes. 'When the user is running, the prosthesis's J curve is compressed at impact, storing energy and absorbing high levels of stress that would otherwise be absorbed by a runner's ankle, knee, hip and lower back,' explains Hilmar Janusson, executive vice president of research and development at Össur. The Cheetah's carbon-fiber layers then rebound off the ground in response to the runner's strides.[29]

This is an example of physical abilities being transformed by a technology, although, unlike the bicycle example discussed previously, it is an example of what could be called an 'assistive technology', a technology that has been designed for people with particular and, in this case, very obvious 'disabilities'. One of the online comments after this article asked the question: 'Would it be fair for a dyslexic youth to win the national spelling bee while using a dictionary because of their difficulties?'

This is an interesting question and refers to someone who has recognised difficulties with reading and writing. But does someone have to be diagnosed as having a 'disability' before we acknowledge the way in which technology could be used to transform their abilities? I cannot imagine, for example, that architects would not use all the resources at hand if they were designing for a competition, including building 3-D models and using a 3-D software program, as well as sketching on paper. Perkins has criticised the way in which education focuses on the individual, drawing attention to this issue by using the contrasting phrases 'person plus' and 'person solo'. He suggests that psychological and educational practices treat the student as a person-solo, allowing the person access to only paper and pencil when asking them to solve an educational assessment task: 'Schools mount a persistent campaign to make the person-plus a person-solo ... and pencil and paper are conceived not so much as thinking aids but as a hopper into which the person-solo can put concrete evidence of achievement'.[30] By contrast, Perkins suggests that if we think of a person as a person-plus, we could then begin to appreciate what this person could do with a set of augmented abilities, abilities that have been transformed by the technological and social resources at hand.

I would turn around the question about a dyslexic youth and ask 'Is it fair that schools do not teach students to transform their abilities with whatever technological or social resource possible?' If schools do not take on this responsibility, then the middle-class child is more likely to learn such possibilities than the child from a poorer background. A middle-class child is more likely to learn to use the Internet to search for and critically engage with information, and more likely to know someone who can offer support with a cognitively demanding activity. Furthermore, parents of middle-class children are more likely to have a child classified as dyslexic in order to harness all the resources that are possible to support such a child to learn and progress at school.

In some respects, a digital technology can be thought of as a prosthesis of the mind, a prosthesis that it may or may not make sense to take away. The phrase 'assistive technology' refers to technologies that have been designed for people with particular disabilities, enabling people to perform tasks that they were formerly unable to accomplish, or had great difficulty in accomplishing.[31] Examples include the use of a hearing aid for a person who has severe hearing difficulties, or the use of Braille for people who are visually impaired. The words 'impairment' and 'disability' have negative connotations and refer to a 'lack' of something. Such a deficit model is often widely used when discussing the reasons why some children might, for example, find it difficult to learn to read when they start school. For example, either their home background might be found lacking or they might be classified as having a learning disorder. However, there is another way of thinking about such situations, and Heinz Wolff[32] coined the phrase 'tools for living' in order to put a positive slant on what might previously have been considered to be aids for the disabled. He makes the point that astronauts in space are disabled by the zero-gravity environment and that technologies are developed to support astronauts, without labelling astronauts as disabled people. He argues that, in a similar way, 'tools for living' should be developed for people on earth, without viewing such people from a deficit model of disability.

Within the education system, technologies are sometimes developed to support the learning process with the expectation that such technologies will eventually be removed (eg software developed to prepare a student for an examination). In such situations, we are interested in the 'effects of' the technology, that is, the effects when we take the technology away.[33] As part of the InterActive Education project, Lazarus developed a use of drop-down menus within a word processor package to support students to start writing in a foreign language. Lazarus was interested in the 'effects of' the use of such drop-down menus, that is, how students would be able to write in a foreign language when they were no longer using this particular digital technology.[34] This is similar to the practice of offering students a 'writing frame' when they are learning to write.

However, in the case of 'tools for living', we are interested in the 'effects with' the technologies, and there is no intention of removing the technology, it continues to be used within everyday practices. In such cases, the technology potentially transforms practice. As long ago as 1985, Pea wrote about the ways in which spreadsheets change the practice of budgeting:

> In terms of the reorganisation metaphor, the tool has restructured the mental work of budgeting. The what has changed: the predominant constituent mental operations for the financial planner are now planning and hypothesis testing by means of interactive development and testing of different models for budgets. The when, or the temporal sequencing, of mental operations in the functional system for budgetary thinking has also changed: now the planner can opportunistically and flexibly test hypotheses in the model virtually wherever and whenever he or she wants. For example, any hypothesis on relationships between cells can be tested by modifying formulas and observing the recalculated results.[35]

This perspective suggests that we are changed by the tools we use; there is a feedback loop by which the very act of interacting with the technology feeds back into our mind and body, so that we learn to do things differently. With artificial legs, it is recognised that a 'disabled' person runs differently. The process of using technologies to transform a person's cognitive abilities is not well recognised by schools and teachers, where the emphasis is often on passing examinations in which the use of technologies are not allowed. I suggest that schools and teachers should find ways of acknowledging that the use of digital tools has the potential to expand cognitive abilities, challenging the traditional view that intelligence is an unchanging attribute of an individual. Rather, intelligence is 'distributed across brain, body and the world looping through an extended technological and sociocultural environment'.[36] As Jenkins points out:

> Teachers have long encouraged students to bring scratch paper into maths examinations, realising that the ability to

construct representations and record processes is vital in solving complex problems. If technologies are inextricably woven with thinking, it makes no sense to factor out what the human brain is doing as the 'real' part of thinking and to view what the technology is doing as a 'cheat' or 'crutch'. Rather we can understand cognitive activity as shared among a number of people and artifacts and cognitive acts as learning to think with other people and artifacts. Following this theory, students need to know how to think with and through their tools as much as they need to record information in their heads.[37]

Capabilities, education and social justice

This chapter is concerned with how digital technologies can be used to transform a young person's abilities, which relates to their potential to participate in society. In order to think more about what this might mean from a social justice perspective, I have found it valuable to draw on Sen's idea of capabilities.[38] The capability perspective provides an alternative to the more dominant economic and human capital perspective on education, which 'tends to view schooling as something like a machine, in which children enter and exit with their human capital appropriately topped up'.[39] By contrast, from a human development and capability approach, the economy is not judged in terms of economic growth, but in terms of 'its capacity to provide opportunities for human flourishing, for each human being to live a life he has reason to choose and value'.[40] A capability approach to education focuses on:

> the ability of human beings to lead lives they have reason to value and to enhance the substantive choices they have.... Concern for human capital should not be neglected as it is alert to the ways in which people develop skills and enhance their income, but earning power and economic values are ultimately not the only dimensions of human flourishing that are important. Education has wider values for individuals beyond enabling them to contribute to economic growth or enhance their own or their families' earning power.[41]

Sen defines a capability as 'a person's ability to do valuable acts or reach valuable states of being. It represents the alternative combinations of things a person is able to do or be'.[42] From this perspective, capabilities are the potential to achieve, whereas functionings are achieved outcomes. Capabilities provide opportunities to achieve and freedom of choice to actively participate in society.

I have argued within this chapter that both technologies and people are available resources that a young person can draw upon when learning and producing in the world. From a social justice perspective, what is

important is how a person converts such resources into capabilities, that is, opportunities to achieve. How a person converts resources into capabilities relates both to the social and cultural context of the use of these resources and to individual difference, agency and choice. It also relates to the personal history of an individual, as well as to what an individual perceives to be possible with the designed technology. But a young person has to learn to convert these human and technological resources into capabilities. And one of the roles of schools is to support young people both to become aware of these possibilities and to develop their own capability set, which relates to their freedom to choose what they would like to be and become. However, as I shall discuss in future chapters, schools and teachers also have a responsibility to develop awareness in young people of alternative possibilities for being and becoming.

As Walker argues, capability refers to what people are able to do and not just to how many resources are available.[43] It focuses on the freedom to be able to choose a life that one values. From this perspective, development is a process of 'expanding the real freedoms that people enjoy'.[44] The idea of agency is central to the capability approach, where agency is viewed as the ability to pursue goals that one values. Diversity is also foregrounded in the capability approach, in that every diverse person is valued by society. Here, the focus on individual diversity should not be confused with the neo-liberal approach to individualism, with its focus on individual self-interest.

Concluding remarks

This chapter has focused on the transformative potential of technologies, in particular, digital technologies, while, at the same time, emphasising that everything we do is situated within a social and cultural context. From this perspective, learning to draw on people in social networks and technologies to transform resources into capabilities is an important aspect of education. I have used Perkins' phrases 'person-solo' and 'person-plus' to emphasise the ways in which schools traditionally focus on the person-solo, whereas in the world outside school, it is the person-plus that is important. From a social justice perspective, I suggest that schools and teachers should support young people to learn how to become effective in the person-plus mode. This could involve young people learning to support each other through peer-group tutoring, young people learning how to search for appropriate information from the Web, young people learning how to use wikis to collectively produce knowledge and young people knowing who to ask for help when they are struggling with a complex problem. In the traditional school system, many of these activities are thought of as 'cheating', and, in this respect, project work and continuous assessment are being removed from high-stakes assessments because of a concern for the ways in which middle-class parents might have more resources available to support their children. In my opinion, the importance of working with human and technological resources should be recognised by schools, this includes recognising the importance of learning to use the resource of a 'more knowledgeable other', learning to work collaboratively and learning to use technologies to enhance cognitive ability and transform what can be produced. The following excerpt from an interview in 2006 with two nine-year-old pupils from a primary school in South Bristol illustrates the potential that is lost when working with others, and when working with digital technologies is considered by schools to be 'cheating':[45]

Interviewer: "Do either of you use Excel at home?" [Alan shakes head.]

Ray: "Sometimes. My Dad uses it for his paperwork."

Interviewer: "And when you use it, what do you use it for?"

Ray: "Umm, he uses it, cos when he's got paper calculations and some are hard like for him, he puts it in Excel and then he puts, he circles it and then presses the equal button and it tells him what the sums are."

Interviewer: "What do you use it for?"

Ray: "Maths homework."

Alan: "Cheat."

Despite a history of computer use in schools, teachers are not embracing the potential of digital technologies for transforming learning, for transforming a young person's capabilities. In this chapter, I have suggested that one of the reasons for this is that in focusing on the achievement of individuals, we downplay the ways in which people and technologies can be harnessed to transform what we can do and become. A view that young people are born into the world with 'fixed abilities' still seems to inform the practices of many teachers, and such a view leads to a culture of low expectations, and also a culture in which the focus is on the person-solo and not the person-plus.

The focus of this chapter has been on the importance of young people learning to convert human and technological resources into capabilities that relate to potential functionings in the world outside school. Within Chapter Three, I turn to the issue of knowledge in the curriculum and argue that enabling young people to engage with and learn about substantive knowledge domains is also an important role of education and schooling.

Notes

[1] Hoyles and Sutherland (1989) and Sutherland (1989).

[2] See, for example, Higgins (2003), Hoyles and Lagrange (2010) and Somekh and Davis (1997).

[3] Pea (1993, p 48).

[4] Herlihy (2004).

[5] See, for example, Boli and Ramirez (1992).

[6] Kutz (2001).

[7] See, for example, Sutherland and Rojano (1993).

[8] Sennett (2008, p 44).

[9.] Sennett (2008, p 41).

[10.] This is referred to as the affordance of a tool or invented thing. Gibson defined the idea of affordance as the action possibilities within an environment, related to the agent and their capabilities. See Gibson (1977, pp 67–82).

[11.] Eagle et al (2008) and Eagle (2012).

[12.] For a discussion of these issues, see Harris (2012).

[13.] Papert S (1980, p 47).

[14.] For information about the Chiltern Logo Project, see Noss (1983).

[15.] See, for example, Facer et al (2003), Holloway and Valentine (2001) and Somekh et al (2002).

[16.] See, for example, Sanger (2001).

[17.] Level 4 is the average level expected of pupils at the end of primary school (aged 10-11). From September 2014 the ICT curriculum will be replaced by computing, with a new statutory programme of study. In the 2014 curriculum the system of using 'levels' to report students' attainment will no longer be used.

[18.] See: www.guardian.co.uk/technology/2011/aug/26/eric-schmidt-chairman-google-education

[19.] Furber (2012).

[20.] Furber (2012, p 5).

[21.] Scratch is a computer programming language developed by Massachusetts Institute of Technology (MIT) media labs for children, which is influenced by the programming language Logo. See: http://scratch.mit.edu

[22.] Speech by Michael Gove, January 2012, www.gov.uk/government/news/harmful-ict-curriculum-set-to-be-dropped-to-make-way-for-rigorous-computer-science

[23.] Jenkins (2009).

[24.] Jenkins (2009, p xiii).

[25.] Source: http://en.wikipedia.org/wiki/Maker_subculture

[26.] Sutherland et al (2008).

[27.] Selwyn (2011a, p 484).

[28.] See: http://en.wikipedia.org/wiki/Edmodo

[29.] Source: www.scientificamerican.com/article.cfm?id=scientists-debate-oscar-pistorius-prosthetic-legs-disqualify-him-olympics

—

30. Perkins (1993, p 95).

31. See: http://en.wikipedia.org/wiki/Assistive_technology

32. See: www.heinzwolff.co.uk

33. For further discussion of this distinction, see Salomon (1990).

34. Gall et al (2009).

35. Pea (1985).

36. Jenkins (2009, p 65).

37. Jenkins (2009, p 65).

38. Sen (2009).

39. Unterhalter (2009, p 789).

40. Unterhalter (2012, p 212).

41. Unterhalter (2012, p 212).

42. Sen (1993, p 30).

43. Walker (2005).

44. Sen (1999, p 1).

45. This excerpt was taken from Sutherland et al (2008, p 175).

CHAPTER THREE

Knowledge worlds: boundaries and barriers

Introduction

This book is being written at a time when new forms of school governance in England are providing schools with the freedom to develop their own curriculum, and within these new structures, some contrasting approaches are emerging.[1] For example, School 21 in Newham London, which opened in September 2012, organises its curriculum around five vital thinking skills for the 21st century: disciplined mind, creating mind, respectful mind, reflective mind and connecting mind.[2] By contrast, the West London Free School, which opened in September 2011, focuses on traditional subjects, with all students in the first three years of secondary school studying Latin.[3] But is the contrast as stark as it appears? These schools have only recently opened and so it is probably too early to say, but in a recent project, we also found contrasts in the curriculum on offer in secondary schools, with some secondary heads arguing for a skills-based curriculum, and others arguing for the importance of subjects, as illustrated by the following quotes:

> "I'm not really bothered how much geography or history they know … because I don't think we should be measuring children's progress in how much they know, because they can access it [on the Web] … this is the 21st century … I think for me what's more important is giving them the tools … so that when they're ready … so actually it doesn't even need such a big touch with the teacher because they've got such good accessibility skills."

> "Now what's the best way forward? I've heard some Principals argue very articulately that it's all about skills. I've heard others argue that if you actually ditch the subjects that is damaging as well … when you actually look at the data at 14, particularly regarding pupils' mathematics skills

> ... then many students might have other skills but they've often gone backwards in mathematics. We've come up with a hybrid for the time being, which is that we keep subjects, but we then try to integrate some of those competencies through the subjects."[4]

These quotes come from a project (the Transition Project) that investigated issues related to the transition from primary to secondary school and it had not been the intention to investigate differences between skills-based and subjects-based curricula. However, as the quotes illustrate, we found that schools expressed very different perspectives about the curriculum at the beginning of secondary school. When we investigated this further, we found that the majority of the secondary schools with a high proportion of students on free school meals had introduced a skills-based curriculum at the beginning of secondary school.[5] Some of these schools had recently replaced predecessor schools that had been in special measures and had been challenged to raise their GCSE results. By contrast, the majority of schools with a more middle-class student intake offered a subject-based curriculum. Whereas it is often argued that a skills-based approach is more similar to a primary school model and will support students in the transition from primary to secondary school, the two fee-charging independent schools in the sample offered a subject-based curriculum at the end of the all-through primary phase (age 9–11) within their schools.

The difference in opinion about the secondary school curriculum also seems to mirror academic debate. For example, Claxton[6] argues that it is skills and not subjects that are key to learning success and expanding young people's capacity to learn, whereas Young[7] maintains that the main purpose of education is for students to gain access to different specialist fields of knowledge.

If there is a social class divide in terms of the curriculum on offer in secondary schools, how does this affect students' life opportunities and potential access to higher education? For example, would a student who did not start to study specialist science until Year 10 find it harder to obtain a place at university to study science than if the same student started specialist science at the beginning of secondary school? How much harder would it be for such a student to gain a place at an elite university? If students have followed a predominantly skills-based curriculum at secondary school, are they advantaged in terms of employment possibilities when they leave school? The 'available curriculum' is clearly an issue of social justice and can be considered to be an aspect of the resources available to young people in school, to be transformed into capabilities that can form the basis for potential functionings in the world outside school.

This chapter, starts by examining the emergence of skills-based curricula in schools and the principles that normally accompany such an approach. It then turns to the work of Michael Young in order to consider the competing ideologies in 21st-century schooling. Following this, I discuss an example from mathematics education in order to look more closely at the potential impact of a skills-based curriculum on the development of knowledge. This leads to a further consideration of the curriculum from the perspective of social justice.

Knowledge and skills in the 21st century

The emergence of what is considered to be a globalised knowledge economy has influenced policymakers to reconsider education from an economic perspective, linked to ideas of 'transformation, modernization, innovation, enterprise, creativity and competitiveness'.[8] An emphasis on innovation, enterprise and creativity also seems to be reflected in approaches to curriculum development, and Morgan suggests that 'curriculum entrepreneurialism' is a characteristic of curriculum development and policy since the late 1990s, and that a range of curriculum brokers have been encouraged to initiate curriculum experiments.[9] Such curriculum initiatives, supported by the Qualifications and Curriculum Authority, tend to be skills-based. Examples include the Paul Hamlyn Foundation's Learning Futures curriculum, Futurelabs' Enquiring Minds curriculum and the Royal Society of Arts' Opening Minds curriculum. Whereas three of the secondary schools in the Transition Project sample were following the Opening Minds curriculum and one was following the Enquiring Minds curriculum, others had developed their own competency-based curricula, one of these being influenced by Claxton's work on Building Learning Power, which focuses on developing learning dispositions, such as resilience, playfulness and reciprocity.[10]

Of these experimental curricula, the Opening Minds curriculum has had the most impact on schools in England.[11] This curriculum focuses on providing young people with life skills or 'competencies', covering five main areas: citizenship, learning, managing information, relating to people and managing situations. Within such a curriculum, young people are able to negotiate with teachers about the content to be learned, and, as such, this is a more 'child-centred orientation where a topic for investigation arises from children's out of school experience'.[12] In the Opening Minds curriculum, the focus is on 'learning how to learn', and the proponents claim that a competency-based approach enables students not just to acquire subject knowledge, but to understand, use and apply it within the context of their wider learning and life. It is also claimed that this curriculum offers students a more holistic and coherent way of learning, enabling them to make connections and apply knowledge across different subject areas.

The idea that young people need to 'learn how to learn' is compelling and I was interested in the perspective of a secondary school head teacher, who we interviewed as part of the Transition Project, whose school had adopted the Opening Minds curriculum. She argued that the students at her school, who drew predominantly from a white working-class area (40% on free school meals and 50% with special educational needs), needed to learn how to become independent learners:

> "So I, personally, think that the starting point for anything is the needs of the children. If the children that come to my school have a specific need, then I think it's up to me to provide that need. If I was in an independent school and had children who were all capable of 10 grade A stars at GCSE, would I be thinking of going down this route? Well, not if it wasn't appropriate for them.
>
> You see, I would argue that what we haven't been good at in this country is actually producing children who can learn independently. And that was one of my big issues here and I tried lots of things – how do I change these children into independent learners? And Opening Minds is the only thing that we've ever really had any success with."[13]

The starting point for this head teacher is the 'needs of the children' (a child-centred approach), and the implicit assumption is that working-class and middle-class students have different needs and thus should experience different curricula. This head teacher has chosen to implement the Opening Minds curriculum in her school because she believes that her students need to learn to become independent learners, and she suggests that such a curriculum might not be appropriate for more middle-class students. However, the Ofsted report for this school, which took place after the interview with the head teacher, suggests that there is a tension between focusing on 'learning how to learn' and learning subjects such as mathematics and English. The report states that the school needs to:

Improve levels of attainment and progress in English and mathematics by consolidating literacy and numeracy developments within the Key Stage 3 'Opening Minds' provision by: creating a stronger link between key competencies and subjects and enriching subject-based vocabulary as a basis for securing conceptual understanding. Some students were constrained because they did not have the subject specific vocabulary they needed across the curriculum subjects to develop their understanding of different concepts. [14]

Of course, it is risky to consider a particular case but this does raise questions for me about the nature of disciplinary knowledge, the subject-specific language linked to such knowledge and the expertise needed in order to teach such knowledge. Alexander has pointed out that the terms 'subjects', 'discipline' and 'knowledge' are not synonymous. A subject is an organisational segment of the curriculum, which may or may not be linked to a discipline, such as mathematics or science. For example, a 'school' subject such as citizenship is not linked to a discipline, whereas a school subject such as mathematics is. Knowledge is central to every discipline and Alexander emphasises that knowledge should not be confused with 'mere facts and information':

The most serious problem here is the equating of knowledge with facts and information. Propositional knowledge is but one kind of knowledge and it is the essence of mature disciplines that propositions must be tested, whether through the assembling and examination of evidence which marks out the methodology of the physical and human sciences or by tests of authenticity and artistry which may be applied in the arts, or simply in relation to honestly-assessed experience. [15]

What is being emphasised in this quote is that domains of knowledge are 'distinct ways of knowing, associated with understanding, enquiry and making sense, which includes processes of inquiry, modes of explanation and criteria for verification'. [16]

By contrast to knowledge, Alexander suggests that a skill is defined as 'the ability to make or do something, especially of a practical kind; requires knowledge but is distinct from it'. [17] Alexander argues that skills are important in education, but that they must complement and not replace knowledge.

Within this section, I have argued that a particular form of curriculum innovation emerged at the end of the 20th century, which tended to foreground skills and background knowledge, deriving from a view that 'knowledge' is no longer important because it can be accessed from the Internet. In general, schools that offer a skills-based curriculum believe that it is important to dedicate curriculum time to explicitly learning process skills, such as managing information and learning to learn. In general, they believe that without such process skills, young people will not leave school equipped to tackle the challenges of the workplace. Curriculum time devoted to the learning of skills usually involves project- or theme-based work, group work, and a cross-curricula approach to learning numeracy and literacy. Another characteristic of a skills-based curriculum is a view that teaching and project-based work should build on students' informal knowledge, which they have developed out of school.

Competing ideologies in the curriculum

Young suggests that recent curriculum policy has been driven by two competing ideologies.[18] The first, called 'neo-conservative traditionalism', centres around the idea of the curriculum as a given body of knowledge that is the responsibility of schools to transmit. This perspective ignores the social and historical nature of knowledge and considers the curriculum to be 'given' and not the outcome of debate and discussion. From this perspective, knowledge learned in school is considered to be superior to everyday knowledge for certain purposes. Such a perspective seems to be reflected in the re-emphasis on traditional subjects within the proposed new curriculum of the Coalition government.

This view is challenged by those who support an ideology described as 'technical-instrumentalist', which centres around the idea that the curriculum should be directed towards the needs of the economy: 'From this perspective, education, the curriculum and even knowledge itself becomes a means to an end and not an end in itself'.[19] Before the 1970s, this perspective on education was restricted to areas of vocational education, but since the beginning of the 1990s, the 'technical-instrumentalist' view has begun to dominate education in general and is aimed at promoting employability for all students.

Young argues that the conflict between the neo-conservative and the instrumentalist perspectives on the curriculum relates to different modes of knowledge production.[20] The neo-conservative perspective views knowledge as insulated and pre-given, whereas the instrumentalist perspective views knowledge as connected and constructed. The first perspective separates general and vocational knowledge, and the second views them as linked. Young argues that the move towards a technical-instrumentalist view of the curriculum relates to a desire to recognise and value knowledge from outside school, where 'pressures for social inclusion require the curriculum to go beyond its traditional subject boundaries and recognise the knowledge and experience of those traditionally excluded from formal education'.[21] Such a perspective is reflected in the move towards a skills-based curriculum in schools.

Young suggests that both ideological positions have not adequately engaged with the ways in which humans participate in the world, creating knowledge and using it to change the world. He introduces the idea of 'powerful knowledge' in order to move away from one of the main critiques of the neo-conservative perspective, namely, that the curriculum being promoted derives from knowledge of the powerful, knowledge of the ruling classes, as was very much the case in England in the 19th century:

> To explore the differentiation of knowledge in the curriculum we need another concept that I want to refer to as powerful knowledge. This refers not to the backgrounds of those who have most access to knowledge, or who give it legitimacy, although both are important issues. Powerful knowledge refers to what the knowledge can do, or what intellectual power it gives to those who have access to it.[22]

Young (drawing on the work of Bernstein[23]) emphasises that knowledge is differentiated in terms of school and everyday knowledge in two ways: first, in terms of the differences between different knowledge domains (eg physics and history); and, second, in terms of the difference between specialist knowledge and pedagogised knowledge (eg school history and history). Underlying these differences, Young points out, is the difference between context-dependent knowledge, which deals with particulars, and context-independent or theoretical knowledge. Context-dependent knowledge deals with particulars that arise in and are learned from everyday life, for example, knowing that different shrubs need to be pruned at different times of the year. By contrast, context-independent knowledge is not tied to particular cases, and refers to knowledge that is codified, and elaborated by specialist communities. So, for example, if I wanted to learn scientific knowledge related to the pruning of shrubs, I might turn to the field of horticulture and learn about the forming of new cell tissue in plants and how cell division works. Young argues that 'context-independent knowledge cannot, except in special cases, be acquired in homes and communities; its acquisition requires curriculum structures located in schools and the support of teachers, with the specialist knowledge and links with universities'.[24]

From a social justice perspective, Young claims that schools have to take the knowledge base of the curriculum seriously:

> The success of pupils is highly dependent on the culture that they bring to school. Elite cultures that are less constrained by the material exigencies of life, are, not surprisingly, far more congruent with acquiring context-independent knowledge than disadvantaged and subordinate cultures. This means that if schools are to play a major role in promoting social equality, they have to take the knowledge base of the curriculum very seriously – even when this appears to go against the immediate demands of pupils (and sometimes their parents). They have to ask the question 'is this curriculum a means by which pupils can acquire powerful knowledge?' For children from disadvantaged homes, active participation in school may be the only opportunity that they have to acquire powerful knowledge and be able to move, intellectually at least, beyond their local and the particular circumstances.[25]

Young is aware that his perspective could be interpreted as supporting the conservative traditionalist approach to knowledge in the curriculum, and this is why he is so careful about the phrase 'powerful knowledge', as opposed to 'knowledge of the powerful'. He emphasises that such powerful knowledge is socially constructed, adopting what he calls a social realist approach to knowledge.[26] This approach to knowledge recognises both the emergent properties and the social basis of knowledge. Social realism aims to move beyond the false dichotomy between a relativist and an absolutist approach to knowledge. Young also acknowledges similarities between this approach and Vygotsky's distinction between everyday and scientific knowledge (to be discussed in more detail in Chapter Four). The idea of 'powerful knowledge' is illustrated in the next section, with examples from mathematics education, and will be returned to in later chapters of this book.

Powerful knowledge: an example from mathematics education

As discussed earlier, a skills-based approach to the curriculum tends to be linked to an approach in which knowledge is taught within cross-curricula projects, an approach in which the boundaries between informal and formal knowledge are blurred and child-centred approaches are valued. In the 1980s, resulting from research that identified children's difficulties with wide-ranging areas of mathematics, there was an emphasis on child-centred approaches to learning mathematics.[27] The emphasis was on building on what children already knew, building on their informal knowledge, in order to teach new areas of mathematics, for example, building on knowledge of addition when teaching multiplication, building on informal trial-and-error approaches when teaching algebra. Very often, children's approaches to solving mathematical problems were celebrated to the extent that new powerful knowledge tended to be de-emphasised. For example, in the example on the right a primary school child has been asked to solve a 'practical problem' about the cost of paving slabs to go around a garden pond.[28] From the diagram, we can see that four square slabs and four rectangular slabs are needed, and we are told that the cost of square slabs is £1.95 each, and the cost of rectangular slabs is £3.50 each.

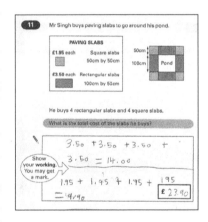

The problem could be solved by the computation 4 x £1.95 added to the computation 4 x £3.50. However, as we can see from the worked-out solution, the student has solved the problem using repeated addition instead of multiplication, and it is possible that this particular student did not know how to perform multiplication calculations. The student has found the correct solution to the problem and some people might argue that this is 'good enough'. However, I suggest that if students do not know how to multiply by the end of primary school, then they have been denied access to powerful mathematical knowledge. Repeated addition may work within this particular problem, but it would be very inefficient in a more complex problem.

Similarly, in the following example, a student has used trial and error instead of algebra in order to solve an 'algebra problem'. Such trial-and-error approaches to solving algebra problems were often encouraged by teachers and were specified in the mathematics curriculum of the 1990s.[29] My own research on algebra found evidence that many students solved 'algebra' problems using a trial-and-error approach, and I argued at the time that these pupils were being denied access to the powerful mathematical ideas of algebra.[30]

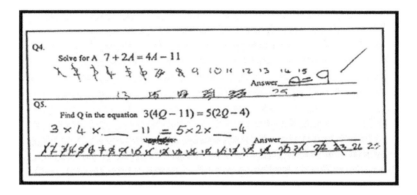

Both of these examples suggest the possibility that the high-stakes assessment system has influenced mathematics teachers to focus on students producing correct answers, instead of focusing on teaching students more powerful mathematics, that is, multiplication and the solution of algebraic equations. My argument is that mathematical knowledge such as multiplication and algebra will not evolve spontaneously from children's own knowledge, and this presents a challenge to both child-centred and cross-curricula approaches to teaching and learning mathematics. In order to 'teach' powerful knowledge such as multiplication and algebra, the teacher has to ensure that students explicitly pay attention to this knowledge. This does not imply a transmission model of teaching, but an approach in which students become aware of the value and power of new mathematical knowledge and appreciate that this knowledge will enable them to solve problems that they would find very difficult with the 'old knowledge'. So, for example, repeated addition may work with the multiplication problem 4 x 3.50, but would be very inefficient with the problem 127 x 0.96. Similarly, trial and error can work when solving the problem 7 + 2A = 4A − 11, but is less likely to work when solving simultaneous equations in algebra.

Through these examples, I am making the case that mathematics as a discipline is an example of powerful knowledge, a domain in which the boundaries between everyday and academic knowledge are differentiated. Most people will probably agree that multiplication is an example of 'powerful knowledge', and that young people will be disadvantaged if they do not learn how to multiply, disadvantaged in terms of their everyday lives and their work, and in terms of progressing to more advanced mathematics. Similarly, algebra provides the background for a sophisticated use and understanding of spreadsheets, and also provides access to advanced mathematical ideas, such as calculus. Moses argues that mathematics education is a civil rights issue and that young people who are not mathematically literate are likely to be disadvantaged in our technological society.[31] My early research relates to this as it was concerned with using digital technologies to introduce students to algebra, students who would have found the traditional approaches to learning the subject challenging.[32]

How to teach a complex knowledge domain such as mathematics involves both understanding the domain and knowing how to transform the knowledge for teaching and learning purposes. I suggest that there needs to be an intention to teach powerful knowledge such as mathematics, and such an intentionality is not likely to be present when the focus is on encouraging child-centred methods, and when the boundaries between everyday and academic knowledge are not appreciated by the teacher.

Curriculum and social justice

In her book *Why knowledge matters in the curriculum*, Wheelahan criticises skills and competency-based curricula, arguing against:

> theories of curriculum that argue that learning should be contextual and situated because this leads to the displacement of theoretical knowledge from the centre of curriculum and in so doing denies students access to the knowledge they need to participate in society's debates and controversies.[33]

She points out that, in most countries, competency-based training is usually located in lower-status, vocationally orientated educational provision and that this is a problem in terms of distributive justice. Her work is influenced by Bernstein, and she emphasises his point that one of the key roles of theory is to 'think the unthinkable and not-yet-thought and to imagine alternative futures'.[34] Wheelahan suggests that access to theoretical knowledge enables students to be part of society's conversations. She makes the same point as Young, arguing that a social realist perspective on knowledge has to be distinguished from a conservative approach in which tradition and authority are the basis of knowledge, as opposed to an emphasis on how the knowledge is produced:

> Education must help students distinguish between theoretical and everyday knowledge by helping them to recognise the boundaries between different kinds of knowledge and to be able to work productively with knowledge ... this is particularly so for working-class students who in contrast to middle-class students do not have extensive family resources to draw on as a second site of pedagogic acquisition.[35]

Knowledge, Wheelahan suggests, has been displaced in vocational curricula, and she also argues that it is being displaced by multidisciplinary problem-solving within academic curricula, in which the context is intended to provide the clues about the type of knowledge needed. The idea that the context can provide clues about the knowledge to be learned has been a dominant element of the mathematical strand of vocational courses in England for some time. For example, in a project in which we investigated the ways in which vocational science students learned mathematics, we found that students invariably used trial-and-refinement methods to solve problems that could have been solved more effectively with algebraic methods and we argued that:

> Without the background knowledge to draw upon to make efficient decisions, many students will continue to be disadvantaged by a system in which the mathematical content is embedded in the vocational context and is expected to be understood through independent learning.[36]

Similar points are made by Rata, who argues that young people who do not develop the ability to separate from their subjective world of experience are restricted from moving into the world of educational achievement:

> A curriculum that provides the knowledge resources for individuals to understand and change their circumstances

is of necessity one that frees people from the limitations of the immediate rather than binding them even more tightly to the subjective world of experience alone.[37]

Young, Wheelahan and Rata all argue that an overemphasis on skills and competencies in the curriculum disadvantages working-class students because in such curricula, knowledge is often underemphasised. Knowledge, they argue, provides access to new ways of thinking, ways of thinking about the unknown, ways of thinking about the not-yet-imagined. So, how does this fit with the idea of capabilities that was introduced in Chapter Two? I suggest that 'powerful knowledge' should be part of a young person's capability set, so that they have the freedom to choose whether or not to use such knowledge. Developing an awareness of the existence of 'powerful knowledge', and understanding that this is qualitatively different from everyday knowledge, is also an important capability to develop.

Concluding remarks

Within this chapter, I have argued that there is a divide with respect to the curricula being offered in schools, with some schools taking a knowledge-based approach and others a skills-based approach. There is some evidence that the curricula on offer are patterned along social class divisions, with fee-charging schools and maintained schools that serve more middle-class areas choosing the more traditional subject-based curriculum. Worryingly it seems as if the old divisions of grammar–secondary modern school and academic–vocational are still pervasive within schools in England.

Whereas it may be the case that many young people from working-class backgrounds need to learn to become independent learners, I suggest that this is not a reason for foregrounding a skills-based approach and backgrounding the traditional subjects. And it is certainly not a reason for differentiating curricula along class divisions. Whereas skills can still be taught within a subject-based curriculum, it is more challenging for 'subjects' to be taught in a predominantly skills-based curriculum. And I do not agree with the point made in the quote at the beginning of this chapter that was essentially saying that knowledge can be reduced to information that can be accessed from the Internet.

Educational reforms of the late 20th and early 21st centuries have been influenced by views about the importance of the market and school choice. But school choice in England is mostly determined by where you live and so in some parts of the country, you may not have the choice of a school that offers a knowledge-based curriculum.[38] Nowadays, despite the rhetoric of school choice, many young people in areas of social disadvantage have almost no choice in terms of access to secondary schools. And if schools with a high proportion of students on free school meals are generally more likely to offer a skills-based curriculum, at least at the beginning of secondary school, then this has to be questioned from a social justice perspective. One of the head teachers we interviewed as part of the Transition Project, whose school has adopted the Royal Society of Arts' Opening Minds curriculum, believes that a skills-based approach is the way forward and that school choice is working against schools in middle-class areas introducing such a curriculum:

> "Now, in many ways – I know it's too simplistic to say this – but parental choice has actually driven the agenda [of the curricula on offer in schools], because the more discerning parents who want the traditional [curriculum], who think it's suited to their children because their children are bright children, choose the schools and, therefore, I know those schools will never change their curriculum to vocational and never consider diplomas because they don't think it's appropriate for their children."[39]

It is worth pausing and studying this statement because it claims that it is parental choice that is influencing the curricula on offer in schools, with middle-class parents demanding a traditional curriculum. If 'middle-class' parents are 'dictating' such a curriculum, are 'working-class' parents choosing and dictating a skills-based curriculum, or are they by default sending their children to schools that offer such an approach, possibly based on a belief by teachers that such a curriculum is somehow more appropriate for their children.

This quote alludes to the way in which a skills-based approach is linked to a vocational curriculum. In this respect, the 'available curriculum' is clearly an issue of social justice and from a capability perspective, can be considered an aspect of the resources available to a young person in school. I wonder if young people and their parents are aware of the ways in which a particular curriculum on offer potentially affects a person's life chances, and that what is on offer in the 11–16 phase affects what you can choose to study in the post-16 phase of schooling. If, as in the preceding quote, a skills-based curriculum is linked to a vocational curriculum, then this suggests that young people in many schools around the country are being denied access to the more academic aspects of education. As Wheelahan argues: 'Unless curriculum is organised so that working-class students and others who are excluded have equitable access to knowledge they will always be on the outside looking in, largely excluded from society's conversation about what it should be like'.[40]

Notes

[1] Although I am discussing the school system in England in this chapter, the issues raised are relevant to changes to educational systems more globally. For a discussion of this, see Ball (2008).

[2] See: http://school21.org/

[3] See: www.westlondonfreeschool.co.uk/

[4] These quotes are taken from Sutherland et al (2010).

[5] Within the sample of 17 secondary schools and their linked primary schools that were part of the Transition Project.

[6] See Claxton (2002).

[7] See Young (2009) and Young (2013).

[8] Ball (2008, p 17). For a criticism of the economic approach to education, see Dorling (2010).

[9] Morgan (2011).

[10] See Claxton et al (2011).

[11] The Opening Minds curriculum was launched in 2000 by the Royal Society of Arts.

[12] See: www.rsaopeningminds.org.uk/about-rsa-openingminds/

[13] These quotes are taken from Sutherland et al (2010).

[14] In order to preserve the anonymity of the school the reference to this Ofsted report is not provided.

[15] Alexander and Armstrong (2010, p 247).

[16] Alexander and Armstrong (2010, p 247).

[17] Alexander and Armstrong (2010 p 251).

[18] Young (2008).

[19] Moore and Young (2010, p 17).

[20] Young (2008).

[21.] Young (2007, p 37).

[22.] Young (2009, p 14).

[23.] Bernstein (1990, 2000).

[24.] Young (2009, p 15).

[25.] Young (2009, p 15).

[26.] See, for example, Maton and Moore (2010).

[27.] For further discussion of this see Sutherland (2006)

[28.] This example was taken from a standard assessment paper that had been completed in 2002 by a pupil (age 10–11) at the end of the primary phase of education.

[29.] Royal Society/JMC Working Group (1997).

[30.] See Sutherland (2007).

[31.] Moses (2001).

[32.] Sutherland (1989).

[33.] Wheelahan (2010, p 1).

[34.] Bernstein (2000, p 148).

[35.] Wheelahan (2010, p 159).

[36.] Butterfield et al (1997).

[37.] Rata (2011, p 17).

[38.] Burgess et al (2010).

[39.] Head teacher interviewed as part of the Transition Project.

[40.] Wheelahan (2010, p 163).

CHAPTER FOUR

Ways of knowing: everyday and academic knowledge

School and home

When I was at school in the 1950s, there were hard boundaries between school and home. At the beginning of secondary school (aged 11), I took a geometry set that had belonged to my grandfather into a mathematics class to show the teacher, and I was severely rebuked for showing off. I can still feel the embarrassment today, and I learned the hard lesson that out-of-school life should be kept separate from in-school life. This raises the issue of the difference between everyday and school objects, between everyday and school knowledge.

A Victorian geometry set carries with it the knowledge of the inventors of geometrical instruments: the protractor, the set square, the pair of compasses. Each instrument has a particular function that relates more to the practical geometry of the Victorian age than to theoretical and academic geometry. Geometry was part of the school curriculum in the late Victorian period, and was still an important part of school mathematics when I was at school in the 1950s.[1]

If the Victorian geometry set is a tool of the Victorian age, what are the tools of the 21st-century digital age? The portable computer, the

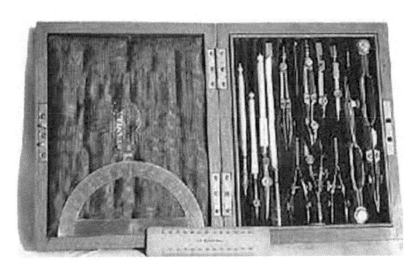

mobile phone, the tablet? Like the Victorian geometry set, these tools are also portable and can be taken back and forth between school and home. But mobile phones are being banned from schools, considered to be disruptive and not relevant to the purpose of schooling.[2] However, schools are more positive about tablet computers and are beginning to experiment with equipping groups of students with such mobile devices for work at home and school.[3] As discussed in Chapter Two, digital devices are multipurpose, they can be used for leisure and for work, for production and consumption, and the more portable and the more multipurpose the device, the more it can be used within every aspect of our lives.

Research has uncovered a variety of ways in which young people use digital technologies in their out-of-school lives, which includes writing for pleasure, playing computer games, using social networking sites and computer programming.[4] There is evidence that young people draw on their out-of-school uses of Information and Communications Technology (ICT) in the classroom, and this can sometimes support in-school learning and is sometimes at odds with what the teacher intends to teach. In the following section of this chapter, I discuss two case studies that focus on young people's use of digital technologies out of school and the relationship between out-of-school and in-school learning. The first explains how 10-year-old Alistair's learning of computer programming out of school influenced his learning of mathematics in school. The second, discusses how a class of primary school pupils' out-of-school experience of computer games was at odds with what the teacher intended them to learn about science. Following these case studies, the chapter introduces Vygotsky's theoretical ideas related to everyday and academic concepts and links this to the work of Michael Young, discussed in Chapter Three. Finally, the chapter ends by making the point that it is not possible to teach academic concepts unless related everyday concepts exist, and the challenging job for the teacher is knowing how to transform everyday knowledge into academic knowledge.

Learning computer programming at home: the case of Alistair

When we first met Alistair, aged nine, he explained how he had become interested in computer programming several years earlier through an after-school club at his primary school. This club was no longer running, but computer programming had become a passionate out-of-school interest for Alistair. He had his own computer in his bedroom (not connected to the Internet as this was before access was readily available), and the window ledge of his bedroom was lined with books on computer programming that his mother had helped him buy from a local bookshop.[5] He lived with his mother and sister in a comfortable home in a semi-rural setting on the outskirts of a large city. He regularly visited his father and her partner, who lived nearby.

Alistair told us that he was interested in writing Basic programs to solve what, for him, were difficult mathematical problems:

Alistair: "And there are some things in programming which you just can't work out with maths, well I've found you can't work out. There aren't procedures that have already been defined to do that, like find a prime number, that would detect if something's a prime number. Then I have to develop my own method of working that out."

Interviewer: "And what method did you choose in the end?"

Alistair: "I made the procedure up myself. It was something like, start with one number, well is it a prime number, you first divide the number by half the number and then round that down to whatever the number is without any decimal places. And then times it by 2 again because you halved the number. If it's the same as the number you want to find if it's a prime, then do something or other, I've forgotten.... First, divide it by 2, round it down to no decimal places and then ..."

Interviewer: "So that would be 3.5 and then 3."

Interviewer: "Oh, so it's testing if something divides into it? Okay, so you're testing to see whether all those numbers go into it, are you?"

Alistair: "Yeah."

Interviewer: "That seems very intriguing, very clever."

Alistair: "Excluding the number itself and 1 because they do divide by themselves."

The process that Alistair used within his computer program is a well-known algorithm for generating prime numbers; although, interestingly, Alistair believed that he had 'invented' the process himself. But, more importantly, Alistair's explanations point to his awareness and understanding of prime numbers, an understanding that he is likely to have developed through his computer programming activities.

We discovered from interviewing Alistair that through computer programming at home, he was engaging with a wide range of mathematical ideas, such as Cartesian coordinates, the difference between integers and decimals, properties of circles, and the idea of variables. This learning of mathematical ideas at home also overlapped with what he was learning at school; although, as he explained to us, it was his father's partner who helped him make the links between mathematics-for-programming and mathematics-for-school. He discussed this when he talked about his end-of-primary-school assessment, where he was the only student to be entered for the highest-level mathematics test:[6]

Alistair: "I'm the only one that did the test."

Interviewer: "And what sort of things were there?"

Alistair: "Um, find the area of the second square if the area of the first square is something or other, something or other, and find the perimeter of these ... I think it was two semi-circles in line and they say find the perimeter, yes. Perimeter? Is that the right word? Yes, perimeter. Um, that sort of thing and algebra."

Interviewer: "What sort of algebra's that?"

Alistair: "Um, mainly equations and that sort of thing."

Interviewer: "For example?"

Alistair: "$Y5 = Y3 + 10$, something like that."

Interviewer: "Y5, why's it called Y5."

Alistair:	"5 times Y."
Interviewer:	"5 Y. Has your teacher told you all this?"
Alistair:	"Uh ... no."
Interviewer:	"How come you can do it then?"
Alistair:	"My dad's girlfriend told me about it."
Interviewer:	"Told you about algebra?"
Alistair:	"Yeah."
Interviewer:	"Why ... is she a maths teacher or something?"

This case study illustrates the type of home–school knowledge exchange that occurred as Alistair moved between the world of home and the world of school. However, Alistair's primary school teacher did not appear to be aware of the mathematics that Alistair was learning through computer programming at home, and was more interested in why he did not use a word processor for homework:

> "But really I don't know what he was using at home and he rarely came to school with work done on a computer, which is quite interesting because his handwriting is appalling. And I really encourage children to use the computers at home for homework. I don't know why he didn't. The only thing I can think of was, you know, that was completely schoolwork and this is home."

There was no awareness or recognition by the school of how computer programming was contributing to Alistair's understanding of mathematics;[7] although, interestingly, his knowledge of mathematics was recognised by the education system, in that he passed the highest possible mathematics level in the end-of-primary-school standardised test.

However Alistair's learning of programming reached a ceiling when he challenged himself to learn how to program in Visual Basic: "My problem is I haven't got like anyone to give me any ideas of actually what to do really" (Alistair). He realised that he needed to work with someone who knew about Visual Basic and appreciated the conceptual gap between Visual Basic and what he had already learned: "You jump across to Visual Basic and there's this giant gaping black void beneath you" (Alistair).

This suggests that whereas it is possible to learn aspects of a knowledge area out of school, there are likely to be concepts within a knowledge domain that are difficult for a student to learn without the support of 'more knowledgeable others'. Alistair was able to learn aspects of algebra, drawing on his knowledge of computer programming and supported by a 'knowledgeable adult' (in the case of Alistair, this was his father's partner), but it was an adult who helped him to transform his programming knowledge into school algebra.

This case study provides evidence of the possibility of learning academic-related knowledge out of school. But the case also illustrates the limits to such out-of-school learning if there is no one at hand who is knowledgeable enough to support the process of knowledge construction. If the Internet had been available, would Alistair have been able to find support from someone at a distance? It is possible, but highly unlikely because the support that Alistair needed required someone who was aware of what Alistair already knew, someone who was sensitive to what Alistair needed to know and someone who had the time to interact with Alistair as he constructed the desired knowledge for himself.

Science simulations and out-of-school game-playing[8]

Nowadays, many young people play computer games out of school and some people argue that game-playing can lead to deep learning.[9] Whatever the value of game-playing in terms of learning, the case study I present in this section illustrates how the focus on 'winning' in game-playing can detract from a focus on knowledge construction. The case study centres around a lesson that was part of a sequence of lessons carried out with 10- to 11-year-old primary students, with the aim of introducing students to the process of scientific investigation. Within each lesson, students were asked to carry out a different scientific investigation using Web-based software. The lessons included both whole-class work around the interactive whiteboard and group-work at the computer. The software VirtualFishtank was chosen by the teacher from a package that came with the interactive whiteboard installed in her classroom, which is available to download for free from the website: www.virtualfishtank.com.

The teacher started the first lesson by showing students how to use the VirtualFishtank software on the interactive whiteboard. This

environment enables the design of a fish with different characteristics (eg size of mouth, position in the tank, likes/dislikes), which is then placed in a virtual fishtank where its survival time before it is eaten by a shark can be timed. The teacher explained that the objective of the lesson was for the students to design a number of fish with different characteristics and then compare how the characteristics of each fish contributed to their ability to survive in this virtual environment before being eaten by the shark. The following is an extract from the beginning of the lesson which shows how the software and the activity were introduced by the teacher.

Teacher: "What we're going to do now is to think about your fish. You are going to design your own fish that you can try and get to live in a particular.... We haven't got an ocean, it's a fish tank ok? What do I mean by the word virtual?"

James: "It's not real"

Teacher: "It's not real, it's like a simulation. So it's a bit of a ..."

James: *"It's a bit like a game."*

Teacher: *"It is a bit like a game."*

...

[Fish died]

Teacher: "So that particular design lasted 2 minutes and 1 second. *I want you to investigate what are the best different types of design to make the best fish to last the longest time."*

...

Jenni: "If it's friendly, it might go up to the shark."

Teacher: "Well this is it, you can investigate, that's it."

...

Teacher: "So, all these predictions that you are making, you've got to change your design and see if those predictions then are true and whether the life expectancy of your fish is actually then increased."

From the beginning, the students interpreted the science simulation as a game, and discussion with the teacher after she watched the video of the lesson suggested that she thought that drawing on the idea of a game would be more likely to engage the students. It is argued by some people that if learning in school were more game-like, then students would be likely to be more motivated and engaged.[10]

After the whole-class demonstration, the students were asked to work in pairs and design their fish. The following are extracts from the discussion of one group of students.

Jessica: "I bet you mine isn't gonna last five minutes. Oh, what's going on? Where's he gone?"

Liam: "Give him food, he's going crazy. He is going crazy. He's getting really thin."

Teacher:	[In background.] "One minute thirty seconds. Well done Marcus. Fantastic."
Sunita:	"Give him some food!"
Liam:	"No let him go. When our fish dies …"
Sunita:	*"Don't die! We gotta beat people."*

The teacher, Sarah Curran, worked with us on a collaborative project aimed at capturing, analysing and communicating the complex interactions between students, teacher and technology that occur in the classroom and after repeated viewings of the video from this lesson, she commented that:

> "I allowed the fun and gaming element of the lesson to become the main factor and lost the learning objectives. The science element became secondary. Part of this was due to not fully knowing the software, but also the way the software looked meant I took things at face value."

The first time Sarah viewed the video-recording, she became aware that the way in which she and the students had engaged with this software in the lesson was at odds with her intended lesson objectives.[11] Although the students had been asked to design several fish, time their survival time and compare their different characteristics, this was not possible because most of the fish survived from 20 to 35 minutes, making it impossible to carry out the investigation in the way that it had been envisaged.

This case study illustrates the way in which students' out-of-school playing of computer games influenced their reading of science simulation software, and that such a 'reading' became a barrier to engaging with the intended science learning. In aiming to engage her students, the teacher unwittingly drew on the students' experience of playing computer games out of school, without realising that this would work against her engaging students with scientific knowledge. This case study contrasts with the previous case study in that in this case, out-of-school activities were at odds with the intended learning. While the students were engaged, they were not focusing on the intended scientific learning. Research as part of the InterActive Education project has shown that teachers often overvalue motivation and engagement, without focusing adequately on what this motivation and engagement is about.[12] This is where analysis of video data of students' interactions in the classroom can enable teachers to pay attention to what the students are actually engaging with and, thus, what they are potentially learning. It was only by analysing the video data that we became aware that both teacher and students were viewing the simulation software as 'gaming' software. When so much is written about the potential of computer games for transforming education, it is perhaps not surprising that the teacher was not aware, until she watched the video-recording of the lesson, that her students would be inappropriately seduced by the gaming aspects of the software.

Everyday and academic concepts

Learning in schools is inevitably influenced by previous learning, whether from out-of-school or from other school learning. As humans, we cannot avoid making sense of the activities we are engaged in by drawing on our previous history of activities and learning. In the preceding case studies, Alistair was able to draw on his experience of computer programming out of school when making sense of algebra in school, and the primary school pupils drew on their experience of game-playing when making sense of a science simulation in school. In this respect, there is an exchange of knowledge between home and school. The preceding case studies, relate to out-of-school uses of ICT but the phenomena is the same for learning with or without digital technologies. For example, young people who learn musical instruments out of school will draw on this knowledge when learning music in school. Young people who watch television programmes about history will draw on these 'histories' when learning history in school.

Learning the language of an academic discipline is an important part of learning about the discipline and very often out-of-school use of language is at odds with the language used within a particular knowledge domain. For example, at the beginning of a lesson on mathematical proof, a group of 13–14 year olds were asked "What is proof?" and one of the students said "When you get school photographs you get those little ones that say 'proof' on them." Proofing or proving is also a term used by professional bakers for the final dough-rise step before baking. Here, the uses of the words 'proof' and 'proofing' in everyday language have different meanings from the use in mathematics. There is research literature that shows how students' (mis)understanding of mathematics can relate to the ways in which everyday language is different from mathematical language,[13] and this is similar within other knowledge domains, for example, physics, history and music. As

Vygotsky argued, concept development is inextricably linked to the development of language, and part of learning a new academic concept involves learning a new 'academic' language. Analysis of the video data in the science simulation case study showed that the teacher did not use any form of scientific language until some 11 minutes into the lesson.[14] In this example, the language of 'gaming' was being prioritised by both the teacher and the students.

Vygotsky and sociocultural theory

I turn now to the work of Vygotsky[15] and sociocultural theory to shed more light on the relationship between everyday and academic concepts. Vygotsky considered that everyday or empirical concepts are developed when children generalise and abstract properties from everyday experiences. This is illustrated by the example of a three-year-old child who observes a needle, a pin and a coin sinking in water and reaches the wrong conclusion that 'all small objects sink'.[16] In this example, what the young child learns from observations is based on the comparison of several different objects or events. Such empirical observation is not likely to lead to the construction of academic concepts (in this case, the concept of density) if the common characteristics of the objects being studied do not reflect their essential characteristics.

Karpov suggests that in school, students are often 'forced' to develop everyday concepts because they are not being 'taught' the academic concepts. This is illustrated by an example taken from my early research on algebra. Eloise, aged 15, was being interviewed about the meaning of letters in algebra and she told me that the value of a letter related to its position in the alphabet. When probed further she provided the following explanation:

Interviewer: "Does L have to be a larger number than A?"

Eloise: "Yes because A starts off as 1 or something."

Interviewer: "What made you think that [L has to be a larger number than A]?"

Eloise: "Because when we were little, we used to do a code like that ... in junior school ... A would equal 1, B equals 2, C equals 3 ... there were possibilities of A being 5 and B being 10 and that

> lot ... but it would come up too high a number
> to do it ... it was always in some order."

Eloise had developed her own theory about the meaning of letters, which derived from her work in primary school, and made sense in the context of the problems she was solving at the time. This knowledge had not been intentionally taught by the teacher, the knowledge had been constructed from Eloise's observations and experience of how letters had been used in particular 'mathematical problems' in primary school. Eloise's knowledge about letters was incorrect from the perspective of algebra, although it was robust knowledge that had survived for many years in secondary school. In order to teach Eloise about the meaning of letters in algebra, a teacher would have to be aware of Eloise's existing conceptions while, at the same time, having the intention of teaching new knowledge.[17] This is the challenge of teaching, which I return to later in this chapter.

By contrast to everyday concepts, Vygotsky argued that academic concepts develop from formal experiences with properties themselves. The focus in the development of scientific concepts is the development of a system of knowledge in which concepts are interrelated:

> theoretical learning is based on students' acquisition of methods for scientific analysis of objects in different subject domains. Each of these methods is aimed at selecting the essential characteristics of objects or events of a certain class and presenting these characteristics in the form of symbolic and graphic models.[18]

Continuing with the example of the scientific concept of density, the science teacher realises that when she asks students why a cork floats in water and a nail sinks, they are likely to answer that it is because the nail is long and thin and the cork is more round:

> Now disconfirming evidence is called for, and the teacher may place a wooden matchstick and a steel ball bearing in the water, clearly challenging the child's naïve concepts by the fact that the match floats and the bearing sinks. At this point however the children are very far from the idea of density, which is a concept that cannot be grasped empirically but requires a theoretical mode of thinking for its appropriation (cf Davydov, 1990). It is one of the concepts Vygotsky called scientific concepts to distinguish

them from the spontaneous concepts children form from their interactions with their everyday environment.[19]

As Steiner and Mahn have pointed out, Vygotsky recognised the interdependence of everyday and scientific concepts, and believed that everyday concepts feed into the learning of scientific concepts and that:

> the dividing line between these two types of concepts turns out to be highly fluid, passing from one side to the other in an infinite number of times in the actual course of development. Right from the start it should be mentioned that the development of spontaneous and academic concepts turn out as processes [sic] which are tightly bound up with one another and which constantly influence one another.[20]

What is important here is that students need some prior knowledge of an area before it is possible to start teaching more systematic academic knowledge. For example, if a primary school teacher wants to introduce pupils to the concept of King, it is important that they already have some everyday notions about this concept, and it is likely that they have encountered the idea of King and Queen from fairy stories, or from watching television. Later, in secondary school, if a teacher wants to introduce students to the difference between monarchy, oligarchy and democracy, then the teacher might start by building on the idea of King developed in primary school, while realising that students are being taught concepts that are qualitatively different from what they had previously learned in primary school.[21]

Vygotsky argued that the 'rudiments of systemisation' are first appreciated by the child through contact with scientific/academic concepts, and that the child then learns to transfer the idea of a system to everyday concepts.[22] In this respect, scientific concepts begin to mediate our practical and everyday experience:

> The relationship, then, between scientific and everyday concepts is dynamic in the sense that it changes, with an initial dependence of scientific concepts on the existence of spontaneous concepts that are themselves transformed in the process of development. By their nature scientific concepts are embedded within a system of interrelated concepts such that their relationship to objects is never direct but mediated by the other concepts that constitute the system, unlike spontaneous concepts that have a direct relationship

with the object and are in this way analogous to empirical concepts. In the process of instruction spontaneous concepts are drawn into explicit conceptual systems of which the child is made consciously aware and over which the child can exercise voluntary control.[23]

The primary question for Vygotsky was what knowledge we want students to learn, and the issue of how to teach such knowledge was a secondary concern. When considering approaches to teaching, the question thus becomes what kind of learning will lead to the development of scientific concepts. Young also makes a similar distinction when he discusses the difference between the curriculum (which refers to the *knowledge* that a country agrees is important for all students to learn) and pedagogy (which refers to how teachers can teach the curriculum), arguing that it is important to separate the curriculum from pedagogy.

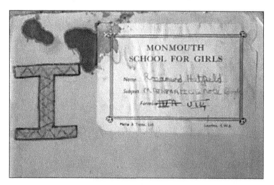

It is beyond the scope of this book to engage with Vygotsky's theory of instruction, although it is important to note that Vygotsky considered that school instruction plays an important role in the development of the child. He also argued that the teaching–learning process is not a one-sided transmission process, but that there is a complex and ongoing relationship between teaching and learning, and that the learning of scientific/academic concepts is inextricably linked to the learning of academic language. He also argued that students actively construct and rework the concepts that the teacher is aiming to teach, and that concept formation only begins when 'the child learns the first meanings and terms that function as their carriers'.[24]

Concluding remarks

Throughout this book, I am making the case that one of the purposes of schooling is to introduce young people to bodies of 'academic' knowledge that they are not likely to bump into out of school. Drawing on the work of Young and Vygotsky, I argue that this knowledge is bounded and is different from spontaneous or everyday knowledge.

This is not to suggest that everyday knowledge is not valuable and there are many situations in which using everyday knowledge is an effective way of dealing with a situation or solving a problem. For example, Nunes has shown how street-sellers in Brazil use efficient 'arithmetic' strategies for solving bartering and money problems. They have learned on the job how to deal with money, but the knowledge they have is different from school mathematical knowledge, and her research showed that these street-sellers were not able to solve school addition and subtraction problems.[25] Drawing on Sen's idea of capabilities (potential functionings), lack of access to knowledge means that we cannot make the decision to use it. The street-sellers in Nunes's study were able to use 'street mathematics' for their own purposes, but they did not have access to 'school mathematics', and so had no choice about whether or not school mathematics would be valuable to them. The research of Nunes and others has been used to 'celebrate' the everyday mathematical skills of unschooled young people, and comparisons have often been made about the relative lack of value of school mathematics. As in the case of my 'unschooled' great-grandparents, I am not wanting to argue that their lives were somehow less valuable than the lives of my family today, but I do want to argue that without being literate and numerate, people have less opportunities and choices about what they can become in life, and that this is an issue of social justice.

Child-centred approaches to teaching and learning celebrate 'everyday knowledge' at the expense of academic knowledge, as I illustrated in the examples of multiplication and algebra discussed in Chapter Three. Child-centred approaches positively encourage experimentation and trial and error, which leads to the construction of everyday as opposed to academic knowledge. Child-centred approaches to pedagogy assume that academic knowledge will develop seamlessly from everyday knowledge. However, academic knowledge does not emerge spontaneously from everyday knowledge and so celebrating or reifying everyday knowledge can become a barrier to the learning of academic knowledge. Everyday knowledge tends to be robust because it 'works' in everyday situations and this is another reason why celebrating everyday knowledge can get in the way of learning academic knowledge. There has to be an intention on behalf of the teacher to teach academic knowledge, and an intention on behalf of the students to learn such academic knowledge.

Vygotsky suggests that it is not possible to teach academic concepts unless related everyday concepts exist, arguing that academic concepts are inextricably linked to everyday concepts. For example, when teaching negative numbers, a mathematics teacher should take into account what students know about these numbers from everyday life (eg weather reports on the television). This out-of-school informal knowledge about negative numbers can inform the teaching of the academic concept of negative numbers while, at the same time, being different from the academic concept. Exceptionally, as in the case of Alistair discussed earlier in this chapter, young people may learn academic concepts out of school, and, in such cases, it is also important for teachers to be aware of the knowledge that the students brings to the classroom.

Alistair worked hard to learn computer programming at home, learning from books and from copying existing programs, but he reached a ceiling in what he could learn without the support of a more knowledgeable other, that is, a teacher. As he explained, he could not manage the "giant gaping black void" between what he had learned about the Basic programming language and what he wanted to learn about Visual Basic. Alistair was from a middle-class bookish family and his mother had bought books to help him with this particular conceptual challenge. Nowadays, Alistair could have joined an online community of computer programmers, but I suggest that such a community would still be unlikely to have provided the support that Alistair needed. The skill of an expert teacher is to understand the student as an epistemic subject, what the student knows already and what the student needs to know. This requires empathy and face-to-face interactions that respond to looks of puzzlement and illumination. This requires dialogue between the teacher and the student that shifts the student into engaging with the new 'desired' knowledge world. Such interactions are hardly possible within online communication. Moreover, for students who are disadvantaged or disenfranchised by the system, 'the opportunity for a meaningful teacher–student relationship is precisely the characteristic that mediates access to academically demanding content'.[26]

At the beginning of this chapter, I talked about how in my early days of secondary school, my mathematics teacher had not been interested in the Victorian geometry set that I had wanted to show her. After this 'rejection', I re-purposed the wooden box into a pencil case, an object that I was allowed to take between home and school. Perhaps this 'pencil case' symbolised geometry and mathematics for me and perhaps my love of mathematics was influenced by the fact that someone at home had allowed me to use my grandfather's Victorian geometry set, recognising my interest in mathematics and enabling me to identify with the geometry of the past. In giving me the geometry set, my father had acted as if I would be able to learn how to use these geometrical instruments, be able to learn geometry and mathematics, launching me into a world of mathematical knowledge.

Notes

[1] Howsam et al (2007).

[2] In May 2012, the new Chief Inspector for schools in England and head of Ofsted called for a ban on mobile phones in schools as a mechanism for tackling disruption and discipline problems in the classroom.

[3] For example, Mount Pleasant School in Penzance has developed a scheme where each student owns a tablet computer.

[4] See for example Facer et al (2003) and Furlong and Davies (2012).

[5] Alistair's mother told us that she had taken her son to the computer science section of the bookshop, Blackwells in Bristol. At the time, this was a large bookshop frequented by university students, but it has since very much reduced and no longer has a computer science section.

[6] He was entered for what is called Level 6 mathematics when in the final year of primary school (Year 6). Approximately 3% of Year 6 pupils in England achieve this level.

[7] The relationship between computer programming and mathematics is recognised in the new computer science curriculum in England.

[8] This section is a reworking of part of the chapter Olivero et al (2009).

[9] See for example Gee (2003).

[10] See for example Gee (2009).

[11] As discussed more fully in Armstrong and Curran (2005).

[12] See Sutherland et al (2008).

[13] See, for example, Durkin and Shire (1991).

[14] Armstrong et al (2005, p 459).

[15] Vygotsky (1978).

[16] Karpov (2003, p 65).

[17] For further discussion of this case, see Sutherland (2007).

[18] Karpov (2003, p 71).

[19] Schmittau (2003, p 226).

[20] Steiner and Mahn (1996, p 365).

[21.] Haenen et al (2003).

[22.] For further discussion of these ideas see Van der Veer and Valsiner (1994).

[23.] Miller (2011, p 115).

[24.] Vygotsky (1986, p 179).

[25.] Nunes et al (1993).

[26.] Panofsky (2003, p 439).

CHAPTER FIVE

Schools as spaces for creating knowledge

A brief history

In the early 1870s, schooling became compulsory for all children up to the age of 13 in England, Wales and Scotland. With mass education came literacy, learning to read and write, and also learning the rudiments of arithmetic. Literacy brings a shift in the way of viewing and interacting with the world. Learning to read 'is in part learning to cope with the unexpressed'.[1] With writing, a dynamic relationship is set up between written and spoken language, turning aspects of language into 'objects of reflection, analysis and design'.[2] Becoming literate enables us to participate in the dominant institutions of society, for example, the legal, the scientific and the religious. The communities that we participate in become textual as well as oral.

It is difficult for me to imagine what life would be like without being able to read and write. My six-year-old twin grandsons are learning these skills at school. They live in a world where everyone around them can read and write, in a world where their parents and grandparents have been reading to them from a very young age. Only four generations ago, my great-great-grandmothers on both sides of my family (from rural Norfolk and industrial Yorkshire) could not read or write. They did not live in families where everyone around them was literate. Nowadays, we are hardly aware of the fact that we live in a 'textual' world, a world where everyday transactions – from ordering shopping online, to filling in a form for a passport, reading road signs and voting – involve interacting with text. With mass schooling, everyone should have the opportunity to learn to read and write.

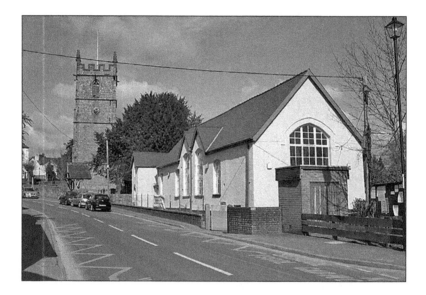

Schools and the buildings that house them are part of the everyday fabric of our world. In cities across the UK, we can still see the Victorian school buildings that were built in the second half of the 19th century, and many of these continue to be used as schools. The imposing Victorian architecture of large inner-city primary schools is somewhat daunting, suggesting discipline and tradition. By contrast, rural Victorian primary schools were much smaller, often only housing two or three classrooms.

Since the building programme of maintained schools at the end of the Victorian era, there have been three waves of school building in the UK.[3] By 1926, primary education became separated from secondary education (at the age of 11) and new purpose-built primary and secondary schools began to be built around the country. In this period, between the First and Second World War, the school leaving age was raised to 14, necessitating extra accommodation, which led to a relatively small building programme. The next wave of school building started in the 1950s to accommodate the increasing number of children born after the war. In England, there was a peak in primary school building in 1954 and a peak in secondary school building in 1958.[4] The Butler Act 1944 created a system of education in which students were tested and streamed at the age of 11 by sitting what was called the 11+ examination. The intention had been to create a tripartite system, with academic schools, technical schools and practical schools. In reality, a bipartite system was created, with grammar and secondary modern schools. Most of the new state-maintained schools built in the 1950s were secondary modern schools, and they were often designed to represent a new and open approach to schooling, in contrast to the Victorian schools. For example, Hunstanton secondary modern school, completed in 1954, 'epitomised the architectural experimentation of post-war Britain, as well as the growing acceptance of modernism by the public authorities'.[5] The school was designed by the Smithdons, two of the most influential British architects of the post-war years. However, the design was criticised from the day the school opened. The huge expanses of glass walls allowed natural light to flood into the classrooms, but also caused the building to overheat in the summer and freeze the students and teachers in the winter. Amy Reynolds, the wife of my

mother's brother, taught in Hunstanton school when it first opened and she was not fond of the building, complaining about the lack of a staff room and the organisation and positioning of the classrooms.

Students who attended secondary modern schools were those who had failed the 11+ examination and so unfortunately these schools became associated with failure. The grammar–secondary modern school divide was predominantly patterned along social class lines, with the majority of middle-class parents whose children did not pass the 11+ examination choosing to send their children to private fee-charging schools. At this time (and the figure is similar today), approximately 7% of young people were educated in fee-charging private schools, some of which are confusingly called 'public schools'. Many of these 'public' schools are very old (eg St Albans School was founded in 948) and are housed in impressive buildings built before and during the Victorian age. In the City of Bristol, for example, just under half of the secondary schools in the city are fee-charging private schools and the majority of these are housed in imposing buildings, opened within or before the Victorian age.

From the middle of the 1960s, comprehensive schools, that is, schools that do not base their intake on selection, began to replace the grammar/secondary modern education system in England, and by 1975, the majority of local education authorities had abandoned the 11+ examination. The majority of comprehensive schools took over what had been secondary modern school buildings. The intention may have been that the new schools designed and built in the 1950s would symbolise light, hope and accessibility, in contrast to the more formidable and traditional Victorian schools. However, by the end of the 21st century, these buildings came to symbolise the failure of both the secondary modern system and the comprehensive education system. This was the case for the predecessor school of the new Academy in South Bristol where I am a governor. By 2008, the building of the predecessor comprehensive school was crumbling, the school had narrowly avoided being placed in special measures and GCSE results were significantly lower than the national average.

By the end of the 20th century, the Labour government of the time led a huge renewal process for secondary schools, with over £1.9 billion pounds being spent on new school buildings before the Coalition government took over in 2010.[6] In this period, over four hundred new secondary schools were built in England, many of these designed by well-known architects.[7] It is difficult to characterise these new buildings: some seem to resemble shopping malls, with their large atriums and walkways; others are designed around a cloister principle similar to an Oxford or Cambridge college; and others are designed as campus schools.[8] Many of these new schools replaced 'failing' comprehensive schools in disadvantaged areas of inner cities. As is the case for Merchants' Academy in South Bristol, there is no doubt that the school designed by the London-based architecture practice Penoyre and Prasad was a first step in creating excellent educational opportunities for young people in the community.[9]

© Tim Soar 2014

It is impossible to say how these new school buildings will be viewed by the end of the 21st century. Hopefully, they will not have fallen into disrepair, as did most of the schools built in the 1950s. Hopefully, they will be more sustainable, more like the buildings of 'elite' schools, which endure over the centuries, with new buildings being added without destroying the old. Whatever the future, this recent wave of school buildings is linked to a symbolic shift in the educational opportunities of young people in England, a shift in the valuing of state education through the acknowledgement of the importance of well-designed spaces for learning. Through such buildings, we have found a way of valuing and respecting 21st-century comprehensive schools. Whatever the criticisms of the Academy programme and the Building Schools of the Future programme, there was no social justice in a system in which schools for the most disadvantaged young people in the country were housed in dilapidated buildings, in stark contrast to the school buildings of the elite schools such as Winchester, Eton and Wellington College.

Schools as institutions

In 1893, all children in England were expected to stay at school until the age of 11. The school leaving age changed to 12 in 1899, to 14 in 1918, to 15 in 1947, to 16 in 1964 and by 2015, it should become

18. Schools appear to be here to stay, but it is important to understand the institutional nature of schools, and in order to do this, I turn to the work of David Olson. Olson argues that schools are more than collections of individuals and that it is important to understand how schools as institutions structure the learning activities of young people:

> A major blindspot in the attempt to create a psychology for education, is the reluctance or inability to grasp, how social institutions structure the social relations between teacher and student as well as the learning and thinking activities of individuals.[10]

Drawing on the work of Tonnies,[11] Olson emphasises the distinction between two categories of social organisation: the Gemeinshaft, a social organisation based on affection and loyalty, such as the family; and the Gesellshaft, a social organisation based on the more formal roles and rules of a modern state.[12] Schools, he argues, fall into the former category of Gemeinshaft, and are institutions with their own rules, with norms, standards, documentation, lines of authority, specialised expertise, credentialing and accountability. Schools have explicit rule-based, textually fixed documentary practices. Schools are bureaucratic institutions that have particular properties, 'that are eventually reflected in the lives and minds of persons that are educated in them'.[13] Schools create categories such as 'ability', 'success' and 'failure', 'hyperactive', and 'differentiation', and these relate to institutional structures, and are not 'natural categories' that exist in a world without schooling.

Olson argues that schools are 'knowledge institutions', and from this perspective, it is important to distinguish Knowledge (with a capital K) from personally held beliefs. Distinguishing Knowledge from personally held beliefs is similar to distinguishing between the institutional organisation of the school and the more informal organisation of, for example, the family. However, Knowledge does not exist separately from those who 'know'. In this respect, knowledge is social and relates to a body of 'knowers' or scientists; Knowledge requires an institution or textual community, it is created through writing and literacy, and the use of documentary practices such as books: 'Writing and printing allowed the development of new forms of social organization that rely less on personal relations and contacts than on roles and rules spelled out in documents'.[14] Truths of institutionalised Knowledge are not absolute truths, but are 'taken as truths', embodied in knowledge institutions, which includes schools.

Olson also emphasises that learning Knowledge requires more than learning the rules of the discipline, it requires learning the feel of the discipline and: 'perhaps most importantly learning how one's personal beliefs and commitments are related to those explicitly expressed in the formal Knowledge of the discipline'.[15] Olson points out that educational traditionalists treat personally held beliefs as Knowledge that must be corrected, often called misconceptions. By contrast, progressive educationalists treat child-centred personal beliefs as privileged. This is a polarisation in terms of building on beliefs (child-centred) and eradicating beliefs (misconceptions). However, such a polarisation is not helpful in terms of advancing education. Olson argues that the transformation of beliefs into Knowledge involves a process of 'explication, formalization, definition, criticism, and most importantly, the norms of institutional judgement'.[16] It is a process of transformation and development, not a process of 'correction' or a process of privileging the personal. In focusing on the conceptual framework of a discipline, we neither discard nor subordinate our own personal beliefs, we transform them. This perspective is similar to Vygotsky's perspective on the difference between everyday and academic knowledge (discussed in Chapter Four).

Emphasising the difference between personally held beliefs and Knowledge is very different from discussions that emphasise personalisation and the blurring of boundaries between home and school. The idea of personalisation has had some influence on visions of 21st-century schooling, and so, in the next section of this chapter, I interrogate the idea of personalisation from a perspective of social justice.

Personalisation and education

Whereas Olson argues that schools are one of the most important inventions of modern society, there are others who suggest that schools are anachronistic institutions, out of step with the modern globalised world. In many of the visions about 21st-century education, 20th-century schools are positioned as conservative organisations that maintain out-of-date forms of authority and curriculum.[17] This is characterised by the story of the time-travelling surgeon and teacher, originally attributed to Seymour Papert[18] and recently retold by Facer:

> In this fable, a mid-nineteenth century surgeon is magically transported through time to a modern operating-theatre. Once there he finds himself at a loss to know what to do or

how to help. In contrast a mid-nineteenth-century teacher is transported through the years to a modern classroom. Once there, he picks up seamlessly where his modern peer left off. The implication of the narrative is clear: unlike medicine, the education community has failed to appropriate the technological advances of the contemporary world.[19]

This tale, often told by people arguing for a new vision of 21st-century learning, is seductive in its simplicity, but misses the point about the relative visibility of technologies for learning in schools in comparison with technologies for surgery. If the key characteristic of schools is that they are institutions for inducting young people into new knowledge worlds, then this is essentially a social process and we would expect people in social relations to be what is most visible in schools, and this does not change much over time. This is very different from the practice of surgery, which uses instrumental techniques to treat a pathological condition or disease. Surgery itself is a technology and so, inevitably, the instruments of surgery are what are most visible and do change over time.[20]

Whereas there have been changes and reforms to the education system throughout the 20th century, the most recent and, arguably, the most forceful call for change has been linked to the advent and integration of digital technologies into our everyday lives. As discussed in Chapter Two, it is the proliferation of personal technologies linked to the Internet that has led to a view that the introduction of technologies in schools is likely to radically change educational practices. The words 'personal' and 'personalised' have gained currency in a range of public services, including education and medicine. In a set of papers on personalising education produced by the Organisation for Economic Co-operation and Development (OECD), there are a range of definitions for what personalised learning means, but they are all similar in that they focus on fitting education to the needs of the individual. For example, Hopkins suggests that personalisation in education means 'matching what is taught and how it is taught, to the individual learner as a person'.[21] Bentley argues that a 'personalised' service reflects the needs and attributes of an individual.[22] And Leadbeater considers personalised education to be similar to tailored services.[23]

In the UK, the principle of personalised learning was launched by the Prime Minister in his speech to the Labour Party Conference on 30 September 2003, and was linked to the policy for introducing City Academies.[24] A few weeks later, David Miliband addressed the National College for School Leadership (October 2003), saying:

The goal is clear. It is what the Prime Minister described in his party conference speech as 'personalised learning': an education system where assessment, curriculum, teaching style, and out of hours provision are all designed to discover and nurture the unique talents of every single pupil ... the most effective teaching depends on really knowing the needs, strengths and weaknesses of individual pupils. So the biggest driver for change and gain is use of data on pupil achievement to design learning experiences that really stretch individual pupils.... Student performance also depends on independent learning. It is inspiring to visit schools where pupils can speak with insight and intelligence about how they learn, about 'mind maps' and other strategies that help them do so, and about those teaching strategies that are also learning strategies that are giving them skills for life. This is the future. Many teachers are committed to it. But in how many schools is there set time each week dedicated for pupils to focus on learning how to learn? In how many schools is assessment for learning designed to support individual target-setting? The answer is not enough.[25]

David Miliband also contributed to the 2006 OECD publication on personalised learning and this text indicates some of the key elements of personalisation as a political strategy of the Labour government of the time. He argued that one of the main challenges of education is 'equity and excellence', suggesting that excellence is often seen as being in opposition to equality. Excellence should be a resource for a more egalitarian educational system and not a threat. The challenge of universality and personalisation relates to a 'demand for high standards related to personal needs'.[26] Personalisation means 'building the organisation of schooling around the needs, aptitudes of individual pupils'.[27] From this perspective, personalised learning is about 'ensuring every pupil achieves the highest standard possible'.[28] Miliband goes on to argue that assessment for learning is an important aspect of personalised learning, and this involves using data to diagnose every student's learning needs. From this perspective, teaching and learning strategies have to build on individual students' needs. The system has to be moulded around the child and not the child moulded around the system.

Ball suggests that one of the organising principles for New Labour's approach to issues of social inequality in education is levels of achievement, and in shifting from a focus on the institution to the individual, there are traces of a new 'IQism', that is, the idea that ability is fixed.[29] It is interesting to consider whether this is the case, and certainly a focus on the individual is very different from the approaches used in some of the countries that have scored highly in international benchmarking tests, where the focus is more on mastery by the whole class as opposed to moulding the system to the student. The issue of mastery, or what Dweck calls a growth mindset, is discussed further in Chapters Six and Seven.

Within the published documents on personalised learning, there is often an implicit criticism of schooling, a re-emphasis of personal needs and a desire to mobilise underutilised resources within the educational system, including young people themselves, families and local communities, what Leadbeater calls the 'untapped potential that lies beyond the school walls'.[30] Leadbeater explicitly criticises what he calls the building blocks of traditional education: the school, the year group, the class, the lesson, the blackboard and the teacher standing at the front of a class of 20/30 children. He argues that all of these aspects of schooling will have to radically change, and, in particular, that a single teacher in front of a class of 30 children cannot personalise learning. He argues that teachers should be able to spend more time designing learning, liaising with parents and advising students on a one-to-one basis. Within such an imagined school, it will be commonplace for older children to teach their peers and younger children. Young people will work in self-managing groups, completing a task together to a deadline. Through such ways of working, they will learn skills in evaluation, analysis, creativity and reflection, and learning to learn. The ideas present in this report are also reflected in the OECD paper by Bentley and Miller, who suggest that family and formal learning will have to become more closely integrated.[31] In such reports, emotional language is used to mount an argument against the status quo. Traditional schools are called 'factories of learning'. The mass education system set up in the Victorian age is under attack: 'The bounded, stand alone school, as a factory of learning, will become a glaring anomaly in this organisational landscape'.[32]

In the personalised learning agenda, it is schools, classrooms and teachers that are under attack, with homes and families and life outside school celebrated as offering additional resources, and young people themselves becoming more skilled at learning how to learn. And although many of the writers about personalised learning suggest that personalised is not the same as individualised, in a study of schools that had taken the personalisation agenda on board, it was found that:

There is considerable evidence in both the case studies and survey that 'personalised' was often interpreted as 'individualised', either in the description of provision made (for example: individual curricular pathways, individual timetables, special arrangements for work experience or accreditation) or in explicit use of the term 'individual' or 'individualised' in responses given to questions.[33]

Personalisation was the dominant theme in a report for the Department for Education and Skills in 2006, linked to a focus on issues of social justice:

Personalisation is a matter of moral purpose and social justice: pupils from the most disadvantaged groups are the least likely to achieve well and participate in higher levels of education or training. Personalisation also reflects wider changes in society, which are likely to continue at an increasing rate. Together, these present the education system with its most acute challenges. They mean that expectations of what all children and young people could and should achieve must be raised, along with schools' capacity to ensure that outcomes for pupils match those expectations.[34]

This report emphasises the persistent attainment gaps between young people from different socio-economic groups. As with other publications on personalisation, a focus on skills is seen as one way of narrowing this attainment gap. The report does not consider what it means to learn about knowledge domains such as mathematics, history and science, although it emphasises the importance of teaching. Interestingly, as I write this chapter, the author of this report, Christine Gilbert, has co-authored a new report on Academies, published on 10 January 2013.[35] A search through the new report for the word 'personalised' produces only two results of little significance. It is interesting to me as an academic who engages and struggles with theoretical concepts that an idea such as personalised learning can completely dominate one report of an author and then several years later hardly appear at all. But perhaps this is not surprising when the phrase 'personalised learning' is very rarely mentioned by the current Coalition government, with its emphasis on traditional subjects in the curriculum. In other words, 'personalised learning' is not a theoretical concept at all, but merely a political slogan that incorporated a mishmash of unrelated ideas that suited a particular political agenda.

If we strip the party-political perspectives from the arguments and attempt to get at the essence of what is important about schools, and, in particular, what is important in terms of education for people from disadvantaged backgrounds, I find myself vehemently disagreeing with the arguments for personalised learning, because they do not engage with the issue of what knowledge is and the idea of schools as institutions for supporting young people to learn knowledge that they are not likely to bump into outside school. Within the personalised learning agenda, there is an intentional blurring of boundaries between outside and inside school, and the use of technology for 'blurring distinctions between informal and formal learning – giving children the ability to choose what they learn and when they learn it'.[36] Some of the rhetoric around personalised learning is laudable, as it argues for young people and parents to become more involved in making decisions related to education, and this is clearly important. However, we are doing parents a disservice if we do not support them to understand the differences between what Olson calls 'personally held beliefs' and 'Knowledge', the difference between what Vygotsky calls 'everyday' and 'academic knowledge'.

In order to return to the issue of schools as institutions in the next section, I discuss three scenarios for future schools developed for Futurelab's Beyond Current Horizons project in order to explore the future of education beyond 2025.[37]

Three scenarios for future schools

In their paper 'Three educational scenarios for the future: lessons from the sociology of knowledge', Young and Muller set out to:

> tell a rather different story about schooling and its possible futures in an increasingly global society. We shall argue that a focus on the conservative nature of educational institutions, their resistance to change, and their perpetuation of anachronistic forms of authority and archaic curriculum priorities that bear little relation to the demands of the contemporary world, is very limited as a basis for 'future thinking'. First, it fails to distinguish between the inherently 'conservative' role of schools as institutions involved in the 'transmission of knowledge' from one generation to another and 'conservatism' as a tendency of all institutions to resist change and preserve the privileges of more powerful groups ... a focus on changes in the wider society, and on how

schools should adapt to them plays down the extent to which, if schools are agencies of cultural transmission, they will have a logic of their own which may go against the immediate demands of young people even if it is in their long term interests.[38]

Young and Muller argue for what they call a 'social realist' approach to knowledge, distinguishing this from an asocial epistemology that 'defines knowledge as sets of verifiable propositions and the methods for testing them',[39] and underemphasises the social production of knowledge. They also distinguish the social realist approach from what they call an 'over-socialised' approach, which 'plays down the propositional character of knowledge and reduces questions of epistemology to "who knows?" and to the identification of knowers and their practices'.[40]

They argue that:

> In contrast, a *social realist* theory sees knowledge as involving sets of systematically related concepts and methods for their empirical exploration and the increasingly specialised *and* historically located 'communities of enquirers' (an idea first expressed by the American philosopher Charles S. Peirce) with their distinctive commitment to the search for truth and the social institutions in which they are located.[41]

Although he does not use the phrase 'social realist', this seems to be similar to what Olson emphasises when he talks about academic or scientific knowledge being constructed through discourse. In discussing a social realist approach to knowledge, Young and Muller are challenging 'the widely shared assumption that boundaries are always barriers to be overcome rather than also conditions for innovation and the production and acquisition of new knowledge'.[42]

The following three future scenarios imagine the future of schooling over the next 20–30 years, taking three different perspectives on knowledge.

In the *Future 1 scenario*, the boundaries between different knowledge traditions are given and fixed and such systems involve 'induction into the dominant knowledge traditions that keep them dominant'.[43] This is the traditional 'elite' system that was dominant in England throughout the beginning of the 20th century and still exists in many schools. This is the view associated with a conservative approach to education, and is being emphasised by the current Coalition government in the UK in its call for a reintroduction into the curriculum of canonical knowledge. Within a Future 1 scenario, knowledge is both ahistorical and under-socialised. Within such a future scenario, teaching is viewed as transmitting knowledge. Young and Muller argue that although this approach to the curriculum still exists in elite private schools and the few remaining grammar schools in England, it has given way in many schools to what they refer to as Future 2, which they call a 'progressive opposition to Future 1'.

In the *Future 2 scenario*, boundaries between knowledge domains and associated school subjects are weakened, as are the boundaries between school knowledge and everyday knowledge. Within Future 2, the idea of expert knowledge is de-emphasised. With the boundaries between subjects being weakened, the curriculum being specified in terms of generic learning-to-learn skills and teaching being viewed as facilitating rather than directing and transmitting. Assessment of the curriculum is usually organised around outcomes or competencies. Young suggests that:

> In its most extreme forms Future 2 argues that because we have no objective way of making knowledge claims, the curriculum should be based on the learner's experiences and interests and that somehow these can be equated with the interests of society.[44]

From a Future 2 perspective, arguments about the importance of knowledge and the boundaries between different knowledge domains are viewed as backward-looking.

In the *Future 3 scenario*, boundaries between school subjects and associated knowledge domains are maintained and boundary-crossing is viewed as the conditions for the creation and acquisition of new knowledge. The Future 3 scenario is based on the assumption that there are 'specific kinds of social condition under which powerful knowledge is acquired'.[45] Such boundaries relate to specialist global communities, for example, the community of mathematicians or the community of historians. Future 3 recognises the conceptual challenges inherent in learning subject knowledge. It also recognises that advances in subject knowledge will be concept-driven, and that:

> new digital technologies will allow forms of investigation that produce facts not previously able to be brought to light and require new conceptual advances. The MRI [magnetic resonance imaging] scans that are driving new advances in neurology are an example. There are parallels

in demography, the Large Hadron Collider in physics and in nano-technology across a range of sciences.[46]

With respect to Future 3, Young and Muller refer to 'powerful knowledge' as opposed to 'knowledge of the powerful' and argue that from this 'social realist' perspective, 'powerful knowledge' is both real and socially constructed. Within Future 3, knowledge within the curriculum is structured and organised as interrelated concepts, which are different from collections of facts. This is an important distinction that is not recognised by those who argue that, nowadays, schools are becoming redundant because young people can access 'knowledge' from the Internet. Young argues that the idea that school subjects are concept-based 'underpins their potential for treating all pupils equally and not as members of different social classes, different ethnic groups or as boys or girls'.[47]

These imagined future scenarios, while necessarily oversimplifying the issues, do provide a way of thinking about future educational possibilities that go beyond the current polarisation between what are considered to be traditional and progressive approaches to education.

I argued in Chapter Two that schooling should be judged by 'its capacity to provide opportunities for human flourishing, that is for each human being to live a life he has "reason to choose and value"'.[48] It is important to keep this in mind at a time when the economic value of education is often the dominant priority of governments around the world.[49] Sen emphasises the importance of an education that specifically encourages critical reflection and the ability to reason in public, and an education that includes traditionally excluded voices. This is a focus on the reflective capacities that enable young people to examine their lives. Such skills, I suggest, are different from the more narrowly focused skills that are considered to have economic value, and are a constituent part of the Future 2 scenario described by Young and Muller.

This chapter has drawn on Olson's idea of schools as enduring social institutions, textual communities with their own rules, norms and specialised expertise, substantially more than collections of individuals. From this perspective, schools are about inducting young people into new Knowledge worlds, and within such worlds, Knowledge is different from personally held beliefs, different from everyday knowledge and different from collections of 'facts'. As such, this perspective resonates with Young's argument for the importance of boundaries between what we learn in the home and what we learn in school, and seems to fit within Young and Muller's Future 3. This perspective is in opposition to the popular call for personalised learning that dominated policy documents in the early 21st century. However, this perspective on knowledge, and the perspective I am arguing for in this book, is also substantially different from the Coalition government's push for returning to traditional subjects in schools (as exemplified in the Future 1 scenario discussed earlier). This is because such an emphasis relates to 'knowledge of the powerful' and not 'powerful knowledge', and does not take into account the fact that knowledge is socially constructed. The perspective I am

arguing for relates to Young and Muller's Future 3 scenario. From this perspective, boundaries between knowledge domains are maintained and boundary-crossing is viewed as a condition for creating new knowledge.

Concluding remarks

Within this chapter, I have begun a process of linking a perspective on Knowledge and schooling to Sen's capability theory, a process that will be returned to in Chapter Eight. In so doing, I am arguing that education is more than an issue of human capital; it is also an issue of 'human flourishing'. I believe that somehow such human flourishing is inextricably linked to the spaces that schools inhabit, and that it is possible to design schools as social spaces that support young people to develop and flourish. Such schools would include both formal and informal learning spaces, and the traditional classroom would still exist, although it might be reinvented as a space for collective knowledge-building.[50] This is a personally held belief and I am not able to argue that it is a 'scientific theory', although it could become a theory (or not) with appropriate research.[51] I also believe that the buildings of the maintained education system need to be comparable with the buildings of the elite education system. This is a challenge when you consider a school such as Magdalen College School Oxford, with its beautiful and extensive educational and sports facilities, clearly visible to passers-by. I can remember walking with my twin grandsons over Magdalen Bridge as I took them for a day out to Oxford's botanical gardens and wondering whether if money were no object, I would want them to attend such a school. Although difficult to resist, if it were my choice, I would have to decline such an opportunity, choosing instead a state school, as I did for my own children. I would recognise that from a social justice perspective, we are already adequately privileged and that young people need an education in which they participate with people from a wide spectrum of society. George Monbiot recently wrote a newspaper article in which he argued that the fact that the vast majority of the current government were educated in elite schools that predominantly cater for the rich and privileged members of society has led to a situation in which this powerful elite is disconnected from the concerns and norms of the rest of society:

> Our own ruling caste, schooled separately, brought up to believe in justifying fairytales, lives in a world of its own, from which it can project power without understanding or even noticing the consequences. A removal from the life of the rest of the nation is no barrier to the desire to dominate it. In fact, it appears to be associated with a powerful sense of entitlement.[52]

I do not want my own grandchildren to be brought up in such a world of power and entitlement, a system that would aim to separate them from ordinary people's lives. But I do want them to have an education in which they have access to 'powerful knowledge' so that they can both participate actively in society and flourish as human beings.

As an endnote to this chapter, I have noticed from an online Ofsted report of Hunstanton School, now called the Smithdon High School, that this school has recently been criticised for its educational standards and its A-level results, and in 2011, was placed in special measures. It interests me that if my mother, Joan Hatfield, were growing up in Norfolk today, she would probably have attended this school. And under these circumstances, it would be very unlikely that she would have passed the necessary academic qualifications to gain access to university. As is nowadays the case for many young people in South Bristol and many other areas of the country, a university education would not have been a possibility for her. That such a situation can exist in the 21st century is, as I have discussed already, a manifestly severe injustice.

Notes

[1] Olson (2003, p 265).

[2.] Olson (2003, p 258).

[3.] For further information about school buildings see Harwood (2010).

[4.] See Seaborne and Lowe (1977, p 155).

[5.] The Open University, The From Here to Modernity Team. Available at: www. open.edu/openlearn/history-the-arts/history/heritage/hunstanton-school

[6.] This money was sometimes linked to the Academy programme, which followed on from the City Technology Programme, and was sometimes part of the Building Schools of the Future programme.

[7.] For example: Norman Foster; Rogers, Penoyre and Prasad; Fielden Clegg Bradley; and Zaha Hadid Architects.

[8.] See Places for Learning, Fielden Clegg Bradley Studios. Available at: www. fcbstudios.com/pdfs/Schools.FINAL.pdf

[9.] Teachers, students and parents are positive about the design of the school, constructed around an inner courtyard.

[10.] Olson (2003, p 48).

[11.] Tonnies (1887).

[12.] Olson (2003, p 37).

[13.] Olson (2003, p 37).

[14.] Olson (2003, p 78).

[15.] Olson (2003, p 72).

[16.] Olson (2003, p 72).

[17.] For a discussion of this issue, see Young and Muller (2010).

[18.] Papert (1993).

[19.] Facer (2011, p 2).

[20.] Personal communication with Andrew Sutherland, surgeon.

[21.] Hopkins (2006, p 18).

[22.] Bentley and Miller (2006, p 117).

[23.] Leadbeater (2006, p 101).

[24.] For discussion of the Academies programme as set up by the Labour government, see Adonis (2012).

[25.] Speech by David Miliband, Minister of state for school standards, to the National College for School Leadership, 22 October 2003. Available at: www. foot-print.co.uk/david-miliband/speech221003.htm

[26.] Miliband (2006, p 23).

[27.] Miliband (2006, p 23).

[28.] Miliband (2006, p 24).

[29.] Ball (2008).

[30.] Leadbeater (2005, p 6).

[31.] Bentley and Miller (2006).

[32.] Leadbeater (2005, p 6).

[33.] Sebha et al (2007, p 66).

[34.] DfES (2006, p 7).

[35.] Academies Commission (2013).

[36.] DfES (2006, p 27).

[37.] See: www.beyondcurrenthorizons.org.uk/

[38.] Young and Muller (2010, p 12).

[39.] Young and Muller (2010, p 14).

[40.] Young and Muller (2010, p 14).

[41.] Young and Muller (2010, p 14; emphasis in original).

[42.] Young and Muller (2010, p 16).

[43.] Young and Muller (2010, p 17).

[44.] Young (2011, p 266).

[45.] Young and Muller (2010, p 19).

[46.] Young and Muller (2010, p 22).

[47.] Young (2011, p 272).

[48.] Unterhalter (2012, p 212).

[49.] For a discussion of this, see Ball (2008).

[50.] For further discussion of this see Sutherland and Sutherland (2010).

[51.] For recent research in this area see Barrett et al (2013).

[52.] Monbiot (2013).

CHAPTER SIX

Assessment and the curriculum in a digital age

Introduction

As I write this chapter, I am aware that there is a major unresolved tension in my thinking about assessment and education. On the one hand, I believe that school league tables have shown up what I called in Chapter One a manifestly severe injustice. An injustice exemplified by the fact that in England in 2011, almost twice as many young people from middle-class homes achieved five good GCSEs (including English and mathematics) than those students from families that were eligible for free school meals (62% compared with 34%).[1] School league tables reveal the existence of schools in which the life chances of the vast majority of their students are severely limited because of their lack of qualifications. They reveal the existence of schools in which the vast majority of students are never likely to have the opportunity to study in higher education.

On the other hand, I also believe that the high-stakes assessment system inhibits the innovation that should be at the heart of improving an educational system. The high-stakes assessment system inhibits innovation related to teaching for engagement with knowledge, innovation related to learning with digital technologies and innovation related to assessment. In this respect it seems to me that the high-stakes assessment system is holding schools back from providing an education that enables young people both to flourish as human beings and to participate in society.

This chapter attempts to unpick this tension in order to investigate whether there are irresolvable contradictions in the system, or whether there could be more constructive ways of moving forward. Suggestions will be made for assessment systems that harness the potential of digital technologies as tools for both constructing knowledge and developing the capabilities for actively participating in society. I will return again to the idea of person-plus in order to suggest that schools should support young people to use both technological and human resources when faced with complex learning situations. I will argue for the importance of teachers continuously seeking feedback about students' learning, and suggest that this is the most important form of assessment in terms of challenging low expectations and enhancing student learning and attainment.[2]

Accountability and challenging low expectations

School inspections and publicly available performance data have shown that some schools are able to succeed against the odds, succeed despite the fact that they serve some of the most disadvantaged communities in the country. The report 'Characteristics of outstanding secondary schools in challenging circumstances' discusses 12 secondary schools that 'defy the association of poverty with outcome'.[3] The report describes the characteristics of these outstanding comprehensive schools, all of which have a higher-than-average proportion of students from families that are eligible for free school meals, and serve communities where few of the population have an education beyond school. The characteristics are summarised as: strong leadership; teaching being consistently excellent; rigorous tracking of progress and timely interventions; the use of student voice; and high expectations of students.

My own experience as a governor of an Academy that opened in 2008 is that in the early years of this Academy, one of the biggest barriers to school improvement was low expectations of what the students could achieve, particularly in mathematics and English. Students arrived in secondary school with low predictions from standardised test data[4] and these predictions were used as 'self-fulfilling prophesies' of what could be achieved by these students. There seemed to be an implicit belief about fixed intelligence, a belief on behalf of many of the teachers that undoubtedly also communicated itself to the students.[5] Any counter-examples that were offered in terms of what it might be possible for these students to achieve were considered not to be relevant for students at this school. In many respects, the school was using data to institutionalise low expectations, and in terms of GCSE results, the school did not make the expected progress in its first two years of opening. For example, if students arrived at the school with a low level of mathematical attainment, they were consigned to a lower set, and expected to make less relative progress in the five years before the GCSE examinations than those who arrived at secondary school with a higher level of attainment. This seems to relate to a view that these students were somehow inherently not able to become highly numerate and literate members of society. Whereas a culture of 'low expectations' is no longer a characteristic of this Academy, I often wonder if progress could have been made more rapidly if the 'low expectations' mindset had been more assertively confronted in the early days of its opening.

By contrast, within the ARK network of Academies,[6] data seem to be used in a very different way. The expectations of students are very high; currently, it is expected that 80% of students attending ARK Academies will obtain at least five GCSEs, including mathematics and English, at grade B or above. The policy in these schools is that those students who arrive in secondary school with a low level of attainment need to make more relative progress in the five years before the GCSE examinations if they are to 'catch up', and a range of interventions are put in place in order to achieve this goal. This reverses what normally happens in secondary school, challenges fixed ideas about ability and social class, and sets up a culture in which young people are expected to succeed against the odds.

The recent report 'A long division' points out that if we want to reverse the trend of low attainment linked to poverty in the UK, then:

> it will not be sufficient for secondary schools to simply ensure that all pupils make equal levels of progress. Rather, they will have to actively target those pupils who are already falling behind when they start out in year 7. Targeting pupils who fall behind in late primary school and early secondary school will be particularly important, as research shows the attainment gap widens very quickly between the ages of 7 and 14 (Goodman et al, 2010).[7]

This report also points out that the role of schools in reducing educational inequality is more challenging at a time when wider social problems prevail, such as poverty and a weak labour market. Moreover, research suggests that only about 20% of variability in terms of student performance is attributable to school-level factors.[8] However, despite these constraints it is important to focus attention on the 'big picture', in which there is evidence that schools can achieve against the odds. From a social justice perspective, reducing the long tail of achievement has to be at the forefront of educational policy initiatives.

So how can schools actively target those pupils who are already falling behind? A recent report by the Sutton Trust[9] provides evidence of those interventions that are likely to have an impact. For example, peer tutoring, in which students work in groups to provide each other with explicit support, is a relatively effective intervention strategy, as is one-to-one tutoring and the use of effective feedback. Interestingly, individualised instruction has not been found to be effective, nor has reducing class sizes.

Although the publication of school league tables and their link to school accountability are widely disliked by many educationists, there is research that suggests that there is a relationship between school effectiveness and the publication of league tables. Simon Burgess and colleagues carried out a natural experiment comparing school effectiveness in England and Wales after Wales discontinued publishing school performance data. They found that school effectiveness in Wales decreased after this change:

> Our results suggest that school accountability policies hold promise for raising school performance, particularly for students in disadvantaged schools and neighbourhoods. If uniform national test results exist, publishing these in a locally comparative format appears to be an extremely cost-effective policy for raising attainment and reducing inequalities in attainment.[10]

The issue of cost-effectiveness is a major factor for those concerned with the economics of education and is one of the considerations when evaluating effective interventions within the Sutton Trust report mentioned earlier. The Coalition government has introduced a pupil premium, which is being allocated to schools on the basis of the number of their students who are eligible for free school meals,[11] and schools have to publish on their websites how they are spending this additional budget. This additional funding will lead to a range of intervention strategies for those students who are falling behind and it has been suggested that:

> Targeted interventions do hold a lot of potential to narrow the attainment gap in schools. A rough estimate suggests that the most effective interventions, such as small group tuition and peer tutoring, could halve the gap between the richest and poorest students if they were implemented effectively. However there are concerns that the design of the pupil premium means it will not be used to maximum effect, and that it will be too narrowly focused on FSM [free school meals] pupils. Policymakers cannot rely solely on interventions funded by the pupil premium to deliver the size of improvements that are required to break the link between poverty and educational attainment.[12]

The 'Long division' report goes on to suggest that it is possible to close the achievement gap in the UK, but that there is a need for more than one-off interventions, there is a need for a system-wide approach. The report argues that closing the achievement gap will require sustained and systematic interventions for all children and young people who are at risk in terms of educational attainment, and, in particular, that investing in early years education is an important factor within such a system-wide approach.

High-stakes assessment and what is valued in the curriculum

I argued in the previous section that in terms of addressing educational inequalities, it is important to be able to compare the performance of schools, and without such comparisons, it is difficult to provide evidence that schools can succeed against the odds. The qualifications for young people in England, normally taken at the age of 16, have become a key factor in the ranking of schools. These qualifications, which include GCSE qualifications and more vocationally oriented qualifications (eg GNVQs and BTECs), have a relatively short history in terms of comprehensive

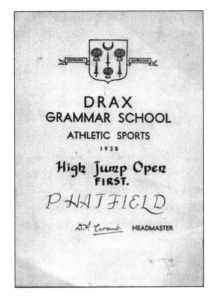

education. Before the introduction of GCSEs in 1988, the examination system for 15–16 year olds was divided into O levels and CSEs, with only 25% of young people taking the academic O level qualification.[13] GCSE qualifications were aimed at overcoming this 'examination divide' and were intended as a qualification for all students, although vocational qualifications have always been available.

Nowadays, the school accountability system has become a super-accountability system,[14] and it is widely agreed that this high-stakes assessment system has negative consequences with respect to the learning experiences of young people in schools: 'Teachers are forced not only to pay attention to results. They live and die by them'.[15] We have reached a position in England where what is valued in the curriculum is synonymous with what is measured, assessed and reported in league tables. There is evidence that schools 'game' the system, as, for example, in the introduction of a wide range of vocational educational qualifications that until recently were equivalent to GCSE qualifications. Alison Wolf addresses this issue in her review of vocational education and recommends that the incentives for schools to 'pile up large numbers of qualifications for "accountability" reasons'[16] needs to be removed. Wolf's report also recommends that a vocational specialism should be confined to 20% of a student's timetable at Key Stage 4, arguing that many vocational qualifications are of no value to young people either in terms of future employment or in terms of access to higher education.[17]

In 2010, the Coalition government announced that the name 'English Baccalaureate' would be used as a new performance measure for schools: 'The measure recognises where pupils have secured a C grade or better across a core of academic subjects – English, mathematics, history or geography, the sciences and a language'.[18] This proposal was heavily criticised by both professionals and academics, the criticism being that the narrowing of focus in terms of the examinations that count towards the accountability of schools will lead to a narrowing of the curriculum on offer to students. Groups that represent religious education, physical education and arts education have all been vociferous in expressing their concerns. Schools have become so good at playing the accountability game that it is very likely that the proposed English Baccalaureate will lead to a narrowing of curriculum focus, and this is most likely to happen in schools that are the most challenged in terms of their examination results, that is, those schools serving disadvantaged communities. In anticipation of these qualifications, there is already evidence that schools are making changes so that subjects such as music and art are less available to students.[19]

It also seems likely that design and technology in the curriculum will be marginalised as a result of the new National Curriculum and the proposed new English Baccalaureate. James Dyson argues that removing design and technology from the national curriculum would be a retrograde step:

> It is a stem subject that uses maths, physics and chemistry and it absolutely deserves to remain as a compulsory subject on the secondary school curriculum.... Without it, it will be even harder to inspire young people to go into the engineering professions and develop new technology. Modern design and technology should sit alongside science

and maths. And it should have the academic rigour of engineering, attracting the brightest minds, and it should be logical, creative, and practical – inspiring young problem-solvers. If you drop DT [design and technology] as a core subject, it will no longer be seen as important.[20]

A recent report for the Design Commission suggests that the government should oppose any move to remove design from the school curriculum, while, at the same time, acknowledging that there is a need to rethink the way in which design and technology currently works as a curriculum subject. The report argues that:

> The point of teaching design to children in school is to teach them that the made world around them – the world of objects, and structures, and environments – is not accidental. It is a compound of decisions that people make. Once you understand that principle, then you begin to have some sense of how these things can be controlled, shaped, made different, changed.[21]

This is very similar to the argument I made in Chapter Two about the importance of designed objects, and the ways in which they can be used to transform human abilities and our interactions with the world. Design and technology was introduced as a school subject in England in the 1980s, and my own children were among the first in the country to learn this subject at school. Having followed a very academic education at my girls' grammar school in the 1950s, I was intrigued by this 'new' subject and thought that it made a very positive contribution to the school curriculum, and in particular to girls' education, because of its focus on manufacturing and engineering. My daughter chose to study architecture when she left school and I wonder if she would have thought that such a profession was a possibility if she had not been introduced to aspects of design at school. At a time when there is considerable enthusiasm for what is called the 'Maker Movement', and excitement about what can be produced by personal 3-D printers,[22] it seems extraordinary that design and technology is losing its claim to be an important and relevant school subject.

Clearly, given what I have argued in previous chapters, I believe that traditional knowledge domains such as mathematics, science and history are an important part of the school curriculum, and so I should be in favour of the proposed English Baccalaureate. However, I am as concerned about a potential narrowing of the school curriculum as are those groups that are currently lobbying the Coalition government. I believe that music and the arts, design and technology, physical education, and moral education are as important as the traditional subject domains. The elite schools in the country are not likely to narrow their curriculum in response to the proposed English Baccalaureate and although the new qualifications have arisen partly to prevent schools from offering students vocational qualifications that are of very little value, the unintended consequences of this new performance measure are likely to work against issues of equity in education. It is even more important that schools with a large proportion of students on free school meals offer subjects such as music in the curriculum, because

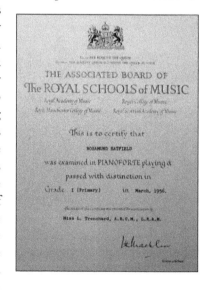

their students are not likely to be having private music lessons out of school, as is very often the case for more middle-class young people.

So, how to get around this impasse? My proposal is that the qualifications that count at age 16 as performance measures of schools should be cut down even further to qualifications in English and mathematics only. This I believe would enable schools to gradually move away from a system in which a subject only 'counts' if it is measured through a high-stakes examination at the age of 16. In many respects, the GCSE examinations are an anachronism in the system, stemming from a time when the school leaving age was 16. By cutting down the accountability measures at 16 to English and mathematics, there would also be a recognition that with the school leaving age increasing to 18, it is the qualifications at age 18 that young people should be working towards. There is a tendency in England for teachers to teach to the level of GCSE, not anticipating the A level courses that follow on from this level. This is even more likely to be the case in schools that do not offer post-16 academic courses, or have only recently become 11–18 schools. The situation seems to be different in other countries, for example, in France, where students know that they are following an academic road that progresses until they leave school aged 18+. Moreover, in Finland, one of the most high-achieving countries in the world in terms of the educational achievements of its young people, there are no mandatory examinations for 16-year-old students. Retaining high-stakes assessment in mathematics and English at age 16 would, I believe, be all that is needed to maintain an accountability system that contributes towards reducing the long tail of achievement in England. As emphasised within Wolf's report, English and mathematics skills are extremely important for entry to the labour market and career progression, and are also important in terms of progression to higher education.

Ofsted inspections could be used to monitor the curriculum in schools and to ensure that all young people, whatever their backgrounds, are offered wide educational opportunities. As Mansell argues: 'a better system would be to have Ofsted inspection reverting to more qualitative verdicts on all aspects of school life, to balance the data obsession of other measures'.[23]

Teaching, feedback and evidence

> The primary function of assessment is to support learning by generating feedback that students can act upon in terms of where they are going, how they are going there and where they are going next. Such assessment involves active student–teacher collaboration, and teachers who also demonstrate that they use assessment in their formative interpretations.[24]

Hattie argues that teachers should view assessment as being feedback on the impact of their teaching, suggesting that there is a need to move from the distinction between what is called summative and formative assessment to 'assessment as feedback'. Hattie bases this claim on his synthesis of over 800 meta-analyses relating to the influences on achievement in school-aged students.[25] I suggest that in England, it will not be possible to move to a situation of 'assessment as feedback' until the high-stakes assessment system of GCSE qualifications (and their equivalents) for 16 year olds is radically changed. This, I believe, could happen if the qualifications that count towards the performance of schools are reduced to qualifications in English and mathematics only. If this happened, a space would be opened up in which teachers and students could experiment with assessment as feedback in the first five years of secondary schooling. There would be no high-stakes assessment barrier to focusing on teaching and learning at the level of the classroom. Hattie argues that the most powerful feedback is provided from the student to the teacher, and that this can be both oral and written feedback. Hattie talks about teachers subscribing to either a 'fixed' or a 'growth' mindset: a 'fixed mindset' relates to a belief that achievement is difficult to change because intelligence is fixed and innate; and a growth mindset relates to a belief that achievement is changeable.[26] It is important for both teachers and students to develop a growth mindset, and Hattie argues that students with such a mindset welcome feedback and are more likely to use it to improve their performance:

> teachers must stop over-emphasising ability and start emphasizing progress, stop seeking evidence to confirm prior expectations but seek evidence to surprise themselves, find ways to raise the achievement of all, stop creating schools that attempt to lock in prior achievement and experiences, and be evidence informed about the talents and growth of all students.[27]

A growth mindset is linked to the idea of mastery, and Hattie argues that all young people can learn when they focus on mastering tasks in a collaborative classroom environment, where there are high levels of cooperation between students and focused teacher feedback that is frequent and diagnostic. In order for teachers to create these conditions in the classroom, they need to believe:

> that their role is that of a change agent – that all students can learn and progress, that achievement for all is changeable and

not fixed, and that demonstrating to all students that they care about their learning is both powerful and effective.[28]

Hattie argues that there needs to be a shift in schools towards supporting students to successfully construct defensible theories of knowledge, away from an over-reliance on surface information. The emphasis here is on teaching and learning particular forms of knowledge, where knowledge is not an unorganised collection of bits of information but a socially constructed and defensible set of interrelated concepts.

Rethinking the digital in assessment

Whereas schools have embraced the digital in the form of data for school improvement purposes, they have not embraced the digital in terms of its transformative potential for students' development and achievement. In schools, there is hardly any recognition of the potential of the digital (as discussed in Chapter Two) as a way of expanding the possible, as a way of expanding a person's abilities. This is completely at odds with person–plus practices in the workplace, practices of musicians, practices of designers, practices of engineers, practices of architects, leisure practices and practices of academics such as mathematicians, scientists and historians. There appears to be an assumption that young people will somehow pick up a person–plus way of working outside school. But, as Jenkins argues, if schools do not teach young people how to exploit the potential of digital technologies, there will be a participation gap, with many young people being disadvantaged because they do not have access to such ways of working outside school.[29]

In 2010, my colleagues and I published a report that emphasised the ways in which the digital could be used in mathematics education in schools. We argued that there is already a wide range of digital technologies that could be used in mathematics classrooms, including: dynamic geometry environments, dynamic graphic tools, algorithmic programming languages, spreadsheets, data-handling software, computer algebra systems and simulation software.[30]

We recommended that 'Curriculum and assessment in school mathematics should explicitly require that all young people become proficient in using digital technologies for mathematical purposes' and that 'High-stakes assessment needs to change in order to encourage the creative use of digital technologies in mathematics classes in schools and colleges'.[31] Interestingly, the role of digital technologies is recognised within a new A level Further Mathematics examination, which focuses on the investigation of curves, functions of complex variables and number theory. Within this examination, each student will have access to a computer with software installed (a graph plotter, a spreadsheet, a Computer Algebra System [CAS] and a programming language), but no communication functionality.[32] The first of these examinations will be held in June 2013.

---

3   (i) Create a program to find all the positive integer solutions to $x^2 - 3y^2 = 1$ with $x \leqslant 100$, $y \leqslant 100$.

   Write out your program in full and list the solutions it gives.   **[10]**

   (ii) Show how the other solutions can be derived from the solution with the smallest x-value.

   Use each solution to give a rational approximation to $\sqrt{3}$.   **[5]**

   (iii) Edit your program so that it will find solutions to $x^2 - ny^2 = 1$, where n is a positive integer. Write out the lines of your program that you have changed.

   Use the edited program to find a rational approximation to $\sqrt{5}$ that is accurate to within 0.1%.   **[6]**

   (iv) Explain why the edited program will not give any results if n is a square number.   **[2]**

Although I am making the case for digital technologies being incorporated into summative assessment for mathematics (because this relates to my expertise), similar cases could be made for other subjects in the curriculum: English, history, design and technology, music, and physical education. For each of these subjects, assessment practices should reflect practices within the discipline outside school, which, in turn, should be reflected within the teaching and learning practices in schools. What is important is that how a knowledge domain is practised, taught and learned should impact on how it is assessed.

The current proposals for the new English Baccalaureate are calling for a timed examination with no technology aids. If, as argued in the previous sections, assessment at 16 is reduced to English and mathematics, other areas of the curriculum could be freed up to develop assessment practices that use digital technologies when appropriate. There would then be an opportunity to creatively develop new forms of assessment that reflect what is important within a domain, for example, composition with digital technology in music, the use of video to analyse sports performances, the use of digital archives for analysing historical evidence and the use of 3-D design packages in design and technology.

There would also be the possibility to experiment with Web 2.0 [33] technologies within assessment practices in order, for example, to use crowd-sourcing as a means of assessment.[34] However, there are a wide range of ethical issues that need to be considered when experimenting with technology-enhanced assessment, for example, the ethical issues linked to the increasing amounts of data being collected and stored. In a recent paper, Patricia Broadfoot, Sue Timmis and I argued that 'Young people should be involved alongside researchers, practitioners and industry members in designing assessment practices that support them to participate in the creation of their own futures.'[35]

Concluding remarks

The aim of this chapter has been to rethink the role of assessment in education. It has been argued that it is important to be able to assess what Perkins calls the person-plus, moving away from the current domination of person-solo forms of assessment. This is clearly a challenge and is in opposition to the Coalition government's exclusive focus on timed examinations in which students are not allowed to use any other resources apart from pen and paper. However, as the example of the Further Mathematics examination paper illustrates, there are ways of allowing students access to digital resources within a timed examination.

I have argued that if the high-stakes examinations at age 16 are cut down to English and mathematics only, then this will leave scope for teachers to experiment with new forms of assessment in all of the subjects in the curriculum, while, at the same time, preparing students for summative assessment at age 18. Such new forms of assessment should involve ways of assessing the group and the class, as well as the individual, while taking into account Hattie's recommendation that assessment should be viewed as feedback on teaching. I argue that the digital should be incorporated into assessment in ways that reflect how the digital is incorporated into practices of teaching and learning, and that experimentation, taking risks and learning from 'failure' are all part of a process of innovation that should be possible within schools.

Finally, I have argued that in order to tackle the manifestly severe injustice exemplified by the fact that almost twice as many students from middle-class backgrounds achieve five good GCSEs (including English and mathematics) than those students from families that are eligible for free school meals, we still need league tables to highlight which schools are achieving against the odds and which schools have an institutionalised low expectation of their students.

Notes

[1.] Clifton and Cook (2012).

[2.] For a discussion of the importance of feedback, see Hattie (2009).

[3.] DfES (2009, p 5).

[4.] When this Academy opened, it made extensive use of the Fischer Family Trust, a charity set up by Mike Fischer, co-founder and former chief executive of RM Education, the education computer company. It provides data analysis for local authorities, and has expanded rapidly in recent years. See www.fft.org.uk.

[5.] Such a belief in fixed abilities appears to be influenced by what is called IQism, treating some children as able and others as lacking in ability. Dorling argues that IQism is 'the underlying rationale for the growth of elitism' (Dorling, 2010, p 46).

[6.] Personal discussion with Helen Drury, Director of Mathematics for ARK schools. See also: www.arkonline.org/home and www.mathematicsmastery.org

[7.] Clifton and Cook (2012, p 19).

[8.] Rasbash et al (2010).

[9.] Higgins et al (2013).

[10.] Burgess et al (2010, p 23).

[11.] See: www.education.gov.uk/schools/pupilsupport/premium

[12.] Clifton and Cook (2012, p 31).

[13.] O level examinations were introduced in the 1950s for those students who were following an academic education. The Certificate of Secondary Education (CSE) was a qualification offered between 1965 and 1987 to those students not following an academic education.

[14.] Mansell (2007).

[15.] Mansell (2007, p 14).

[16.] Wolf (2011, p 11).

[17.] Wolf (2011, p 11).

[18.] In January 2012, the government announced that computer science would be added to this list. See: http://education.gov.uk/schools/teachingandlearning/qualifications/englishbac/a0075975/the-english-baccalaureate

[19.] Greevy et al (2012).

[20.] As reported in *The Guardian* (2011).

[21.] Design Commission (2011, p 27).

[22.] See: http://en.wikipedia.org/wiki/Maker_culture and http://en.wikipedia.org/wiki/3D_printing

[23.] Mansell (2007, p 249).

[24.] Hattie (2009, p 126).

[25.] Hattie (2009, p 126).

[26.] For discussion of these concepts, see Dweck (2012).

[27.] Hattie (2009, p 124).

[28.] Hattie (2009, p 124).

[29.] Jenkins (2009).

[30.] JMC (2011).

[31.] JMC (2011, p 6).

[32.] Mathematics in Education and Industry (MEI) Further Pure Mathematics with Technology, see: www.mei.org.uk/?page=fpt

[33.] Web 2.0 refers to the second generation of World Wide Web tools that allow collaboration and open sharing of information (for example Twitter, Facebook).

[34.] See Jones and Alcock (2012).

[35.] Broadfoot et al (2013, p 1). Available at: www.bris.ac.uk/education/research/sites/tea/publications/index.html

CHAPTER SEVEN

Education in the 21st century

The purpose of education

I have argued throughout this book that education should be about developing the capabilities that enable young people both to flourish as human beings and to participate in society. I have also claimed that one aspect of this development relates to entering new knowledge worlds, worlds that provide access to 'powerful knowledge'. However, being educated is not only about oneself, it is also about recognising others as 'persons worthy of respect'.[1] This perspective on the purpose of education is much wider than the perspective that has been dominant since the end of the 20th century, namely, a view that education is about developing the skills that will enhance economic growth.

Education, then, is about more than gaining qualifications, although these are also important and, from a social justice perspective, all young people should have the opportunities to gain the qualifications that a society values. When the school leaving age in England becomes 18, the qualifications that a young person achieves within the 16–18 phase of education will be crucial in terms of opening up a lifetime of opportunities. Such qualifications should enable a young person to progress into the world of work, into an apprenticeship or into higher education. The possibility that many young people may not be aware of what post-16 qualifications offer was brought home to me recently when I interviewed 13-year-old Sarah as part of the evaluation of the Future Brunels programme, designed to encourage young people to become scientists and engineers.[2] Sarah is a confident young girl who is doing very well at school and has embraced the opportunities being offered by the project. She is clearly someone who could go to university, if this is what she chooses. Her parents left school at 16, and she lives in a community where the majority of people also left school at 16. When I asked her a question about whether she wanted to study A levels she replied:

> "Yeah. If it gets me like better in life, then I'll do it … like if it gives me more of a chance to get like a better job or something. I don't really understand what are A levels. I

know what they are, but I don't know like what they give you."

This response shows that Sarah knows that A levels exist but that she has no awareness of what they offer, and this is not surprising as these qualifications are beyond the experience of her parents, her brother and the wider community in which she lives. It has to be the responsibility of the school to educate Sarah and other young people like Sarah about what A levels and other post-16 courses offer. Sarah's secondary school has only just started to offer academic courses at this level, and, with time, the culture is likely to change so that knowledge about what the sixth form offers will permeate throughout the school. However, we should be shocked by the fact that in the 21st century, and after almost 50 years of comprehensive education, there still exist young people who have very little knowledge about post-16 qualifications, and thus very little knowledge about how such qualifications could lead to employment and higher education possibilities.

While qualifications are important, I argued in Chapter Five that the current high-stakes assessment system has distorted the work of schools, and, in particular, the schools that are most scrutinised, the schools that serve the most disadvantaged communities. Schools urgently need to move away from what Coffield calls 'exam factories',[3] and provide the space for students to engage with substantive knowledge, knowledge that enables them to think the unthinkable and imagine alternative futures. I suggested in Chapter Six that one way forward is to cut back the examinations that count, at age 16, in terms of performance tables to mathematics and English qualifications only. I believe that this would enable teachers to experiment with new forms of teaching and new forms of assessment, moving away from an emphasis on rote memorisation of facts and moving towards a focus on 'powerful knowledge'. As I have argued throughout the book, knowledge is more than bits of information and collections of facts. Moreover, knowledge worlds are bounded, and academic knowledge is qualitatively different from everyday knowledge. High-stakes assessment has contributed to a fragmentation of knowledge into bits of information, and, at the same time, the rise of the Internet has led to a view that such fragmented knowledge can be accessed electronically. I suggest that it is important to understand school knowledge as 'academic' knowledge that is organised around coherent, connected and complex collections of concepts,[4] and, from this perspective, knowledge cannot be readily accessed from the Internet. Hattie also argues that there needs to be a shift from an over-reliance on surface knowledge to students creating theories of knowing, suggesting that an emphasis on the reproduction of surface knowledge relates to teachers wanting to maximise students' achievement in examinations.[5]

As I emphasised in Chapter Five, becoming literate is a key aspect of schooling and education, enabling a young person to participate in society and gain access to the institutions of society. People who are functionally illiterate are likely to remain at the margins of society. Although I appreciate that becoming literate in a digital age involves engaging with digital as well as non-digital texts, I am cautious about overemphasising new forms of digital literacy[6] because I believe that paper-based forms of literacy are still important aspects of education and schooling.

This chapter starts by considering the ways in which humans construct theories as part of their everyday lives. With this as a starting point, the chapter then discusses a range of folk theories about pedagogy, introducing what Olson calls a future pedagogy that enables teachers to support students to move beyond their personal and everyday knowledge to construct knowledge that society 'takes as known', to construct 'powerful knowledge'. I then suggest that knowledge objects themselves can either be digital or non-digital, and that people can actively expand their capabilities through awareness of the possibilities and constraints of particular knowledge objects. I continue by discussing the ways in which educational systems tend to attribute either psychological or sociological factors to a student's performance, ignoring the role of students themselves as being responsible for their own education. This leads to a discussion of the role of teachers and teaching, and finally to a call for the establishment of a UK body to unite teachers as a profession, a body that is able to champion the importance of the quality of teaching.

Theory as a way of seeing

> Humans are irrepressible theorisers. We can't help but note similarities among diverse experiences, to see relationships among events and to develop theories that explain these relationships (and that predict others).[7]

As the preceding quote emphasises, humans are irrepressible theorisers, we construct theories as we interact with the world. These everyday theories are intuitive and implicit – personally held beliefs and the language we use to communicate them often reflect such beliefs. For example, if we talk about a person 'having' a particular ability, then the use of the word 'have' relates to a metaphor of possession, and this links to a belief that people possess abilities that are invariant, that cannot be changed by education and schooling. Such language is likely to link to what Bowles and Gintis called IQism, that is, a belief that there are inherited differences in intelligence.[8]

What is important here is the idea that through our everyday interactions with the world, we construct personal beliefs or folk theories and these folk theories inform our ongoing behaviour and actions. For example, if teachers believe that ability is fixed, then they are not likely to be able to embrace what Dweck calls a growth mindset,[9] namely, that abilities can be developed through work and persistence. If teachers believe that the construction of knowledge should be the result of the child's own enquiries (a child-centred approach), then they are not likely to accept the idea that there are boundaries between everyday and academic knowledge.

A theme running throughout this book is the importance of distinguishing between everyday and academic knowledge, between personally held beliefs and Knowledge with a capital K. My argument is that the work of the teacher in confronting their own everyday folk theories is similar to the work that teachers have to do with their students, in supporting young people to shift from everyday to academic knowledge. And I suggest that such a meta-level approach to theory should pervade all aspects of education and schooling, including the professional development of teachers.

Knowledge and pedagogy

Olson and Bruner argue that: 'Beliefs or assumptions about teaching, whether in a school or in any other context, are a direct reflection about the beliefs and assumptions that the teacher holds about the learner'.[10] In order to draw attention to different views about the relationship between teaching and learning, Olson identifies four folk theories about pedagogy. The first of these he calls 'imitation and learning to do', and suggests that this is the dominant folk theory within non-literate and non-bureaucratic societies, where learning is left 'largely to the innate imitative and agentive resources of children, allowing them to have whatever beliefs they find interesting and useful, so long as they comply with the largely implicit social norms of the society'.[11] Within this pedagogy, learning is not reduced to teaching, and learners take responsibility for their own learning. He also suggests that this type of learning is central to learning in the pre-school years.

The second folk theory Olson calls 'the acquisition of knowledge', and this is characterised by teachers presenting students with facts, principles and rules of action. This is a 'transmission' pedagogy, which 'took precedence when large-scale dominating institutions, whether the church or the nation, took certain beliefs and forms of action as central to their growth or survival and created institutions, primarily schools, to see that these patterns were preserved'.[12]

The third folk pedagogy Olson calls 'the acquisition of beliefs', and he suggests that this child-centred folk pedagogy arose from a criticism of the 'acquisition of knowledge' pedagogy. This third folk pedagogy 'flowed from republican and democratic nations in which the individual was granted the right to play a role in the formation and control of the state'.[13] The perspective here is that institutions, such as schools, serve young people rather than dominate them. From this perspective, knowledge is not seen as objectively given and true, but as a human invention.

Olson suggests that psychological theory for the past century has battled between the second and third folk pedagogy:

> that is the teacher tries, often unsuccessfully to mediate between the rigid standards of the published curriculum, and the feasible achievements of each child. In so doing, the teacher switches between these two pedagogies, often feeling guilty about either ignoring the ministry guidelines or accommodating the special needs of the child.[14]

Olson argues that there is a way out of this polemic, by 'setting out a framework for relating private felt understandings with explicit, objective criteria specified by the institutional forms, the disciplined knowledge'.[15] This fourth pedagogy acknowledges the existence of 'a cultural store of socially sanctioned knowledge that has been constructed by means of accepted procedures and monitored by the knowledge institutions of the society, roughly "what is taken as known"'.[16]

Central to the idea of a fourth pedagogy is the concept of 'joint intentions', and of fusing 'private intentions' with 'joint intentions'. From this perspective:

> the teacher neither completely accepts responsibility for student knowledge, as in the second folk pedagogy, nor simply turns the responsibility over to the learners, as in the third folk pedagogy. Rather it is a pedagogy of arriving at a joint goal, both shared and public, against which either student or teacher can assess his or her performance and take corrective action.[17]

Olson suggests that within the fourth pedagogy, the pedagogical exchange may be divided into two phases: the first relates to agreeing on a joint goal; and the second to developing a means for reaching that goal.

I have chosen to discuss Olson's four pedagogies in some detail because I believe that the fourth pedagogy, which Olson also calls a 'future pedagogy', begins to address the challenges of teaching young people 'powerful knowledge' and moves away from the flip-flop polarity between the second (traditional) and third (child-centred) folk pedagogies. The fourth and future pedagogy distinguishes between what Olson calls personal beliefs and Knowledge, and what Vygotsky calls everyday and academic knowledge.

The idea of the teacher and students establishing a joint learning project, and joint pedagogical intentions in which teacher and students agree on the norms and institutional standards for performance, and in which students engage with the knowledge traditions of a discipline, is I believe a productive way forward that leads out of the impasse between traditional and child-centred pedagogies. It recognises that:

> acquiring disciplinary knowledge is learning to cope with and participate in the powerful institutions of the society, through understanding the basic theory of those disciplines and the reasons and evidence on which they are based, even if they are somewhat discrepant from one's own privately held beliefs and commitments.[18]

In the fourth pedagogy, teaching and learning are not considered to be separate acts, the focus is on the system, a system in which there is one teacher and many students, a system in which it is acknowledged that knowledge is socially constructed.

It is not possible within this book to pursue Olson's idea of a fourth pedagogy in more depth, although I suggest that there are similarities here with the Activity theory branch of sociocultural theory and what Engeström means when he discusses the importance of teacher and students establishing a jointly shared 'object' within what he calls 'expansive learning'.[19] Engeström argues that expansive learning is an inherently multi-voiced process of discussion, negotiation and orchestration, and is a way out of the polarisation between an acquisition-based approach to knowledge (what Olson calls pedagogy 2) and a participation-based approach to knowledge (what Olson calls pedagogy 3). As Engeström points out:

> Acquisition-based approaches may ostensibly value theoretical concepts, but their very theory of concepts is quite uniformly empiricist and formal (Davydov, 1990). Participation-based approaches are commonly suspicious if not hostile toward the formation of theoretical concepts, largely because these approaches, too, see theoretical concepts mainly as formal 'bookish' abstractions. So the theory of expansive learning must rely on its own metaphor: expansion. The core idea is qualitatively different from both acquisition and participation. In expansive learning, learners learn something that is not yet there. In other words, the learners construct a new object and concept for their collective activity, and implement this new object and concept in practice.[20]

It also seems to me that there are some similarities between what Olson calls a fourth pedagogy and what Bereiter calls knowledge work. Bereiter argues that one aspect of classroom-based knowledge work is the creation of epistemic artefacts, conceptual tools that serve in the further advancement of knowledge. From this perspective, the role of the teacher is to support students to transform their subjectively held beliefs into theories that stand up in the 'public market place of evidence'.[21] From a knowledge work perspective, abstract knowledge objects, such as theories, numbers and designs, should be accepted as:

> real things outside the mind, which people may develop relationships with as they do with animate and inanimate material things. Understanding and mastery may be treated as characteristics of such relationships, and the advancement of knowledge as the creating and improvement of conceptual artefacts.[22]

In Chapter Five, I suggested that the idea of a teacher with a class of students is under attack by people who believe that the educational system is no longer fit for the 21st century. This perspective tends to link to a belief that skills are more important than knowledge, and that knowledge can be readily accessed from the Internet. Often implicit in this belief is the view that one-to-one teaching is the ideal situation, and that education would be transformed if only a tutor for every child could be found.[23] However, the idea of one-to-one teaching does not take into account the fact that knowledge is socially constructed through discourse and interactions within a community. From a sociocultural perspective, 'language is the master tool' that permeates all our interactions in the world[24] and learning a new knowledge domain involves developing the language practices that are associated with that particular knowledge domain.

How, then, can young people learn the different languages that relate to different knowledge domains? Drawing on the work of Bakhtin, Wertsch uses the word 'ventriloquation' to describe the process by which we learn to speak with a new language. We learn new words by 'copying' and appropriating the words used by other people. In order to speak, we do not learn words from a dictionary; rather, we learn them from 'other people's mouths'. This is not to say that we completely 'parrot' someone else's language, we creatively adapt the words and language of others.[25] In order to appropriate the language of a new knowledge world, we need to hear this language spoken, and this is why the teacher plays a crucial role in inducting young people into the language practices of a particular knowledge world. Teachers do this by being aware of their role as gatekeepers of new knowledge worlds, by using the language of the knowledge practice and by supporting students to shift to new language practices, for example, the language of chemistry, the language of mathematics, the language of history or the language of music.

Knowledge in a digital age

One of the central ideas of this book, influenced by sociocultural theory, is the idea that all human action is mediated by cultural, social and cognitive 'tools', that is, all human action involves interaction and dialogue with multiple 'knowledgeable others' and with multiple tools and technologies. In Chapter Two, I discussed the idea of technologies and tools that can be used to transform a person's capabilities, focusing on the idea of person-plus. Whereas the focus in Chapter Two was on digital and non-digital technologies, Bereiter argues that 'knowledge objects' can also be considered to be powerful tools that potentially transform what a person can do and become, that is, tools that mediate action.[26] From this perspective, a knowledge object could be represented either digitally or non-digitally, and there is a blurring of boundaries between digital tools and knowledge tools, and also a blurring of boundaries between the digital and the non-digital. In other words, engagement with a knowledge world is mediated by the 'objects' of that knowledge world and such objects could be digital or non-digital. For example, geometry could be represented non-digitally on paper or digitally within a dynamic geometry environment. Composition in music could be represented as a non-digital musical score on paper or as a digital composition.[27] And within many knowledge domains, data are increasingly represented digitally, for example, within astrophysics, economics and geography.

Wertsch argues for the importance of incorporating the idea of a 'toolkit' within sociocultural approaches to teaching and learning:

> If we incorporate the notion of a tool kit into Vygotsky's approach, action continues to be shaped by mediational means but several new questions arise: what is the nature of the diversity of mediational means and why is one, as opposed to another, mediational means employed in carrying out a particular form of action.[28]

A toolkit approach relates to the idea that it is important to discriminate between the potential of different tools, the potential of different knowledge objects. Why, for example, is multiplication more powerful than repeated addition for solving particular problems? This involves considering the relative potential of a particular knowledge object for a particular purpose. Wertsch introduced the word 'privileging' to refer to the fact that a particular tool can be viewed as being more appropriate or efficacious in a particular setting. For example, Matthewman argues that mono-modal language is the most effective tool for critically reflecting on multimodal texts.[29] Wertsch suggests that differences between people can be understood as being related to how they 'recognise and create contexts by using various items from a tool kit',[30] by contrast with the view that differences between people relate to what could be called 'ability'. In this respect, a 'toolkit' approach relates to the idea of a person actively expanding their capabilities through awareness of the possibilities and constraints of particular technologies and particular knowledge objects.

Agency and responsibility

> Who is responsible for children's learning? Clearly no one
> can learn for the child; that is something the learner has to
> do for him or herself. But who should take responsibility
> when children fail? Traditional explanations of success
> and failure appealed to the IQ and the social class of the
> children themselves. Modern reform efforts under the label
> of accountability have pointed the finger at the teacher,
> but then also to the school, and even to the policymakers
> and directors of education. Seeking accountability in either
> source ... has obscured the most important of all educational
> resources, namely, the learner's sense of agency and his or
> her sense of responsibility for learning.[31]

In the preceding quote, Olson suggests that schools and the educational
system have not been paying enough attention to the most important
aspect of educational resources, namely, the students themselves.
He argues that psychology absolves students from responsibility for
their own learning by its focus on dispositions that are not within
their control, such as mental abilities and personality dispositions (eg
Attention Deficit Hyperactivity Disorder). He argues that the social
sciences absolve students from responsibility through a focus on social
constructs, for example, parental background, social class, race, gender
and poverty. And he argues that high-stakes testing and assessment
regimes have taken the responsibility away from students and placed
it on teachers and schools. He says that:

> By diverting responsibility for learning to the myriad
> agencies outside the child, the child has been left as a subject
> rather than an agent. This is where the accountability train
> left the tracks; concern for accountability ends before it
> reaches its rightful subject, the learner him or herself.[32]

The way forward, Olson argues, is through the practice of the future
pedagogy, discussed in an earlier section of this chapter. From this
perspective, joint intentions represented in a shared language provide a
bridge between what is 'taken as known' within a society and the beliefs
and intentions of students themselves. The fourth pedagogy 'allows the
learner, ultimately to take responsibility for his or her own learning
of the society's legitimated knowledge'.[33] The fourth pedagogy starts
with a joint responsibility between teacher and students to negotiate a

shared goal and 'The teacher's responsibility is not to convince the child but to form a joint intention to entertain the proposition and second to examine evidence, that is reason for belief'.[34] Within the process of negotiating a joint intention, language is used to make promises, a form of social control, and in this respect 'Speech acts learned through making commitments to others become devices for regulating the self. Speech acts, then, become the route to taking on responsibility for present action and planning for the future'.[35]

Within such a process of negotiation, the student's and teacher's actions are mediated by language, where language is the 'master tool'. As I have discussed already from a sociocultural perspective, all human activity is mediated by tools, both social and technological. Whereas I agree with Olson's assertion that students themselves must take responsibility for their own learning and education, I also argue that students should become aware of the ways in which they can expand their capabilities through the use of technologies and through working with people. The idea of responsibility is also central to Sen's theory of capabilities, and he argues that 'freedom to choose gives us the opportunity to decide what we should do, but with that opportunity comes the responsibility for what we do – to the extent that they are chosen action'.[36]

There is a risk that in re-emphasising the responsibility of students, teachers themselves could then view themselves as being absolved from responsibility (Olson's folk pedagogy 3). However, within Olson's fourth pedagogy, the teacher is responsible for creating the social conditions within the classroom so that students are able to engage with and construct powerful knowledge for themselves.

Teachers and teaching

> "Some teachers, you know, pound it into you, try to just get information into you, they don't get anything back, that's a bad teaching manner, I don't like that type of teaching at all when the teacher just gives you information and says 'Write it down' bla bla bla 'This is it. Revise from it.' That's not good teaching at all. Good teaching is when the teacher asks for questions from the class and answers the questions that the kids give, you know. That's good teaching. But when they just give you information and that's it, they don't answer questions, they don't let you involve yourself in the lesson, that's not a good type of teaching, that's really bad teaching." [37]

The preceding quote comes from an interview I carried out with a 13-year-old boy some years ago. Huw explains why he thinks that good teaching involves a two-way system and bad teaching involves one-way transmission of knowledge. He also suggests that bad teaching relates to an emphasis on revising for examinations.

Hattie claims that teachers have to believe that they are:

> evaluators, change agents, adaptive learning experts, seekers of feedback about our impact, engaged in dialogue and challenge, and developers of trust with all, and then we see opportunity in error, and are keen to spread the message about the power, fun and impact that we have on learning.[38]

If the teacher that Huw was referring to had taken such an enquiry-based approach to his teaching, he might have learned from the perspective of his students, learned that students value dialogue as opposed to monologue. If the purpose of schooling is to develop young people's capabilities to participate in society, then such capabilities are developed at the level of the interactions between teachers and students, at the level of the classroom. Whether teaching students how to play basketball in physical education, geometry in mathematics or composition in music, expert teachers differ from novice teachers in how they organise the knowledge to be taught, in how they engage students with this knowledge.

As I discussed in Chapter Six, feedback or formative evaluation is the most powerful form of information that a teacher can have in terms of knowing about their impact on student learning. Hattie argues that teachers should actively seek information about their students' learning, using assessment as feedback. However, he claims that knowing what is optimal does not mean having a set of rules to follow, but making decisions 'on the fly', during the class. Here, the focus is on the interactions between the teacher and students, and the evaluation of learning from the perspective of the students.

Hattie emphasises the importance of teachers believing that success or failure in student learning is about what they as teachers do:

> This proposition is not making the claim that students are not involved in the equation, or that all success or failure is indeed the responsibility of the teacher; rather it is claiming that the greatest impact relates to the teacher's mindset. Within this mindset a positive belief on behalf of the teacher that needs to be fostered is there is no deficit

thinking – that is there is no labeling of students, nor are there low expectations of students.[39]

Is there a tension between what Hattie is saying here and the issues I discussed in the previous section, related to the importance of recognising that students are responsible for their own learning? I think not, because although Hattie emphasises the role of teachers as potential change agents, that is, the people who can make a difference through the expectations they have of students and through the ways in which they work in the classroom, Hattie also recognises the responsibilities that students have for their own learning. As Olson points out, teachers are not responsible for student learning, but they are responsible for providing opportunities for students to learn.

I suggested in Chapter Six that one of the main factors that holds schools back in terms of student achievement is low expectations of students, and that the uncritical use of attainment data can feed into and fuel such low expectations. Teachers can draw on a wide range of evidence to inform classroom practice, using both qualitative data (eg video-recordings of a lesson, interviews with students) and quantitative data (eg diagnostic assessment). Such evidence can be used to expand views about what students can learn, contributing to an understanding of teaching and learning within a particular knowledge domain.

I suggest that part of becoming an expert teacher is developing awareness of personal folk theories, challenging personally held beliefs and transforming such beliefs into what could be called evidence-informed knowledge and practice. In this respect, an important aspect of professional development for teachers is making folk theories explicit and developing new theories that are influenced by both bodies of knowledge about teaching and learning, and also critical reflection, experimentation and evidence.

Teachers as professionals

The professional serves one other, often neglected purpose. He or she interprets and translates the goals of the institution into classroom activities in such a way that students can for themselves take responsibility for their learning.[40]

In a recent book, *The allure of order*, Jal Mehta argues that schooling and education in the US has become increasingly regulated and that the perceived failure of schools has led to increased levels of control of schools and teachers. He suggests that the situation in the US is in stark contrast to the situation in countries that are considered to have successful educational systems, for example, Korea, Japan, Canada and Finland. In such countries:

> they choose their teachers from among the most talented students; they train them extensively; they provide opportunities for them to collaborate within and across schools to improve their practice. They provide the needed external support for them to do this work well; and they support this educational work within stronger welfare states.[41]

While not wanting to attribute success to all of the factors listed within the previous quote, Mehta makes the point that, in general, the educationally successful countries take a very different approach from that taken in the US. Whereas the control-oriented strategy taken within the US might be appropriate when work is highly routinised and standardisable, it is not appropriate, Mehta argues, when work is complex and non-routine, as is the case for teaching within schools. Here, a more professional structure for the workforce would be a better organisational form.

Within the book, Mehta puts forward a number of propositions for how the practice of teaching should change so that it grows from practice out, and this includes the suggestion that knowledge about teaching and learning needs to be created 'by those closer to the site of practice', that is, by teachers themselves. He also argues that, in his vision, 'Schools would present the outcomes of professional development work to one another, sharing the lessons they've learned rather than relying on experts on high'.[42]

Within his proposed remodelled system, the first step would be to develop practice-relevant knowledge, the second would be recruiting talented practitioners and the third would be creating schools that are centres of inquiry, and that this:

> would be a significant shift from the compliance mentality that characterizes 'top-down' reforms. It asks teachers not to be implementers of ideas drawn up by others but rather active participants, working together to develop teaching ideas and solve problems of practice.[43]

I suggest that if Mehta had analysed the English educational system, he would have drawn similar conclusions. In England, schools and teachers are becoming increasingly controlled and although performance measures and inspection regimes change, the drive is always in the direction of controlling from the centre. The middle level of control, namely, the local authority, is increasingly being disempowered and the school system is becoming fragmented, with a proliferation of standalone schools and chains of Academies.[44] This has led some people in England to suggest that the time has come for teaching to become a self-regulated profession similar to medicine and law. For example, in an article in *The Guardian* on 22 April 2013, Estelle Morris suggested that:

> A professional body might, however, be an idea whose time has come. It may not yet be a talking point in staffrooms, but there is a growing consensus for an organisation such as a royal college of teaching. There has been a view for some time that the absence of an independent body to regulate standards and oversee professional practice makes teaching less of a profession than, for example, medicine or nursing. This is still a persuasive argument, but the present policy landscape makes the proposition more compelling than ever. A royal college would be a uniting force that would bring the profession together around common standards and shared professionalism.[45]

Notes

[1] Pring (2013, p 38).

[2] See: www.ssgreatbritain.org/about-us/press/introducing-trust's-12-new-'future-brunels'

[3] Coffield and Williamson (2011).

[4] For an extensive discussion of this, see Davydov (1990).

[5] Hattie (2009).

[6] For a discussion of digital literacy, see Dobson and Willinsky (2009).

[7] Davis et al (2000, p 52).

[8] Bowles and Gintis (1976, p 119).

[9] Dweck (2012).

[10] Olson and Bruner (1996, p 11).

[11] Olson (2003, p 222).

[12.] Olson (2003, p 222).

[13.] Olson (2003, p 222).

[14.] Olson (2003, p 221).

[15.] Olson (2003, p 223).

[16.] Olson (2003, p 224).

[17.] Olson (2003, p 225).

[18.] Olson (2003, p 288).

[19.] Engeström (2003)

[20.] Engeström and Sannino (2010, p 2).

[21.] Bereiter (2002, p 77).

[22.] Bereiter (2002, p 179).

[23.] The idea of developing one-to-one tutors is also dominant in some branches of technology-enhanced learning, see, for example, 'One informed tutor per child', in Fischer et al (2013).

[24.] Cole and Engeström (2010, p 2).

[25.] For further discussion of this, see Wertsch (1991, p 127).

[26.] Bereiter (2002).

[27.] See for example Gall and Breeze (2005).

[28.] Wertsch (1991, p 94).

[29.] Matthewman (2009).

[30.] Wertsch (1991, p 96).

[31.] Olson (2012).

[32.] Olson (2012).

[33.] Olson (2003, p 250).

[34.] Olson (2003, p 248).

[35.] Olson (2012).

[36.] Sen (2009, p 19).

[37.] Interview with 13-year-old boy as part of Economic and Social Science Research Council (ESRC) Screenplay project; see Facer et al (2003).

[38.] Hattie (2009, p 159).

[39.] Hattie (2009, p 159).

[40.] Olson (2003, p 235).

[41.] Mehta (2013, p 269).

[42.] Mehta (2013, p 204).

[43.] Mehta (2013, p 279).

[44.] For an explanation of what is meant by academy chains see NCSL (2012).

[45.] Morris (2013).

CHAPTER EIGHT

The idea of justice in education

Introduction

Recently, in my role as governor of a secondary school, I was asked to sit on a panel with teachers to interview the students who had applied to continue studying in the sixth form. As a member of the panel, I asked each student what they would like to be doing in five years' time. One girl said that she wanted to become a palaeontologist; a boy said that he wanted to become a professional darts player. Others said that they wanted to become a journalist, a lawyer, a car mechanic, a physical education (PE) teacher and a professional footballer. I wondered if all of these opportunities were open to them and what subjects it was best for them to study in the 16–18 phase of education in order for them to be able to achieve their goals. Would the girl who wanted to become a palaeontologist be disadvantaged because she cannot currently study physics at A level in this particular school? What about the student who wants to become a PE teacher? Would he be in a good position to gain a place at university on an appropriate course if he studies a vocational (BTEC) national diploma in sport or would it be better for him to study an A level PE course? I also wondered whether the subjects that they had studied already in the pre-16 phase of education

would put them in a good position to realise their aspirations.[1] For example, would the young person who wants to become a doctor be disadvantaged by her 16+ examination results, as it is very competitive to gain a place at medical school? Some of these young people had chosen to study vocational subjects as part of their pre-16 courses and I was aware of Alison Wolf's claim that students are studying vocationally related qualifications:

> for reasons which have nothing to do with their long term interests within education or the labour market. They can and do find that they are unable, as a result to progress to the courses they want and have been led to expect they will enter.[2]

All of the students that I talked to had ideas about what they wanted to become and I get angry when people say that young people such as these, from working-class backgrounds, are not aspirational. But what is different about these young people in comparison with those from more middle-class backgrounds is that they may not have studied the appropriate pre-16 courses and may not be able to study the appropriate post-16 courses that are needed in order to realise their aspirations. And, importantly, these young people and their parents may not be aware of the situation that they are in.

The set of capabilities that these young people have developed through their education may not give them the freedom to realise their aspirations. In order to explore this issue further, this chapter starts by returning to the idea of capabilities, discussing what practical actions could be taken in order to address issues of social injustice. I suggest that one practical action is for schools within a local area to work together, and this leads, in the next section of the chapter, to a discussion of the importance of cooperation between schools, and between students within a school. I then move on to discuss the importance of cooperation in terms of the professional development of teachers and discuss a way of working that involves academics and teachers working together, an approach to professional development that was developed within the InterActive Education project.[3] I then move on to discuss the provocative proposals put forward by Andrew Adonis about how fee-charging private schools could become more integrated into the state-maintained school system in England. Finally, I end the chapter and the book with a personal reflection on the pleasure of making and writing, and a personal reflection on how to take practical steps to reduce the severe injustices that continue to exist within the educational system.

Capabilities and the 'opportunities to become'

The idea of capabilities is deceptively simple and yet enigmatically powerful. The idea of capabilities centres around the question 'What should be the set of opportunities or substantial freedoms that people may or may not exercise in action?'[4] This set of opportunities is the capability set available to a person. The idea of capabilities is linked to the idea of the 'opportunity to become'. Within the idea of capabilities is respect for people to have the freedom to decide what they want to do or become. So, for example, we should not place a value judgement on whether an individual chooses to study at university, but, at the same time, all young people should have the opportunity to choose whether or not to study at university. And unless a young person studies particular courses and obtains particular qualifications at school, the opportunity of progressing to university is not available. Thus, an important part of the idea of capabilities is that a person has choice with respect to the way in which he or she transforms capabilities into what are called functionings. In this respect, the focus is on 'comprehensive opportunities' and not on what happens as 'culmination'. Walker and Unterhalter provide an example of the difference between capabilities and functionings:

> Two 13-year-old girls in Kenya participating in an international study of learning achievements fail mathematics. For one, despite attending a well equipped school in Nairobi with qualified and motivated teachers offering ample learning support and a safe learning environment, a major reason for her failure was her decision to spend less time on mathematics and more time with friends in the drama club and other leisure activities. For the other, from a school in Wajir, one of Kenya's poorest districts, despite her interest in mathematics and school work, her results were largely due to the lack of a mathematics teacher at her school.[5]

For both of these students, the functionings are the same, they both fail their mathematics examination, but the capabilities for each student are different: 'The capability approach requires that we do not simply evaluate the functionings, but the real freedom or opportunities each student had available to achieve what she valued'.[6]

The idea of capabilities centres around a comparative methodology. It focuses on comparative assessments as opposed to identifying a transcendental solution: 'this relational rather than transcendental framework concentrates on the practical reason behind what is to be chosen and which decisions should be taken, rather than speculating on what a perfectly just society would look like'.[7] Sen argues that the idea of justice can be advanced by comparing what people can realise, what he calls a realisation-focused comparison. In making such comparisons, he argues that we should allow for incompleteness in social assessments, recognising 'the inescapable plurality of competing principles, and that alternative perspectives may be in conflict with each other'.[8] Such an approach can allow us to compare different groups in society, as I have done by comparing the educational opportunities for young people in North Bristol with young people in South Bristol. This comparison reveals that the opportunities to study academic courses before 16 are more restricted for young people in South Bristol, the opportunities to obtain at least five GCSE examinations including mathematics and English are more restricted, and the opportunities to continue education post-16 are more restricted. For all of these reasons, the opportunities for young people to progress to higher education in South Bristol are vastly different from the opportunities for young people in North Bristol. This is an injustice that relates to social class, to inequalities within society and to poverty.

The capabilities approach foregrounds the identification of injustice and then proceeds through 'reasoned diagnosis of injustice to the analysis of ways of advancing justice'.[9] Dialogue and communication are all important aspects of the capabilities approach to justice. From this perspective, I suggest that in Bristol, and in other similar cities, all citizens have a collective responsibility to identify ways of advancing educational justice. It could be argued that this should be the responsibility of the local education authority, but in the city of Bristol, the local authority has not made much progress when dealing with the severe educational injustice that has persisted for at least 20 years. However, it does not help to blame the local authority, or blame the fee-charging private schools in the city, or blame individual schools or blame the politicians. What, then, is a way forward? Could all the schools in the city, the two universities, the business organisations, the local councillors and the recently elected mayor agree that something should be done about these severe educational injustices? Is there a way for all these stakeholders to work cooperatively together to analyse ways of advancing educational-related justice in the city? In order to begin to answer this question, in the next section of this chapter, I look more closely at what it means to cooperate.

Cooperation between schools and between students

I argued in the last section that we have to take a collective responsibility when tackling the manifestly severe injustices that exist with respect to education in England. And a starting point is a collective responsibility at a local level, for example, at the level of the city of Bristol. This is clearly a challenge, and many subgroups in a city such as Bristol have worked hard for years in pairwise cooperations aimed at tackling the educational injustices within the city, with only relatively small effects when examined from a top-down perspective. Is this because of the inherent competition within the system, for example, the competition between different private fee-charging schools, the competition between fee-charging and state-maintained schools, and the competition between the two universities? Is this because of a lack of respect between different players within the city, for example, between the local authority state-maintained schools and the new Academies, and between the business sector and the local authority?

I suggest that such a collective responsibility has to engage with the tension between competition and cooperation. Sennett suggests that in the UK (and in the US), the school system has been developed around competition, and he points out that there is both a lack of cooperation between schools in these countries and a lack of cooperation between young people within the schools. He suggests that there is more cooperation within the school system in Scandinavian countries and Far East countries, such as China and Japan.[10] These countries, he says, have found a better balance between competition and cooperation. For example, Chinese children spend more time on learning in groups, and Japanese mothers spend more time than British mothers in helping their children study. He also suggests that the social consequences of economic inequality can be counterbalanced in 'capitalist societies with strong family cohesion, in schools that emphasise the value of studying seriously together'.[11] Sennett makes a strong point that in children's lives, 'inequality relates to sociability and more practically to cooperation',[12] adding that he believes that 'online sociability' is not enabling young people to cooperate and socialise across class lines, and that the deep bond of duty to cooperate (what the Chinese call '*guanxi*') is not something that is likely to occur online. There are two important points here: the first is the possibility that online social networks exacerbate class divisions in society; and the second is that we are not likely to be learning the difficult skills of cooperation through online social networking.

Sennett argues that people's capacity for cooperation is much greater than institutions allow and that cooperation is a skill that can be learned. He draws on the work of Sen and Nussbaum[13] in order to argue that cooperation should become part of a young person's capability set. He also argues that cooperation should not be put into opposition with competition, and that both can exist, describing a number of scenarios in which it is possible to learn the balance between cooperation and competition, for example, playing a team sport.

For Sennett, cooperation is a skill, and he argues that learning a skill relates to craft work. This is an interesting position from the perspective of education, where the idea of craft is linked to vocational education, which continues to be positioned as being different from academic education, and which has a history of not being valued within the English education system. For Sennett, there are three interrelated sub-skills to be learned when learning how to cooperate. Drawing on the work of Bakhtin,[14] he argues that the first of these skills relates to dialogic communication, and the importance of attempting to take in what people mean, to hear what is not spoken and to dwell on ambiguity. Within dialogic communication, there is an acceptance that it might not be possible to reach a common understanding. By contrast, the focus within dialectics is to develop a common understanding. The phrase that Bakhtin used to help the understanding of the idea of dialogic communication is 'knitted-together but divergent exchange',[15] and Sennett says that this is similar to musicians playing jazz, each bouncing off one another. The second skill relates to the use of informal speech when working together, and the use of the subjunctive, which Sennett suggests 'is at home in the dialogic domain'.[16] He suggests that when we use the subjunctive mode of speech, we leave space for others to participate, inviting 'the other to lay out different kinds of responses'.[17] The third skill that relates to learning how to cooperate is the skill of empathy, that is, paying attention to something that you cannot understand. Sennett contrasts empathy with sympathy, which is becoming aware of someone's needs by identifying with them and trying to understand them:

> Sympathy overcomes differences through imaginative acts of identification; empathy attends to another person on his or her terms. Sympathy has usually been thought a stronger sentiment than empathy, because 'I feel your pain' puts the stress on what I feel; it activates one's own ego. Empathy is

a more demanding exercise, at least in listening; the listener has to get outside him- or herself.[18]

I have spent some time describing what Sennett suggests are the sub-skills of cooperation because I have for many years been influenced by Bakhtin's idea of dialogic speech[19] and have drawn on some of these ideas in work on teachers' professional development, to be discussed in the next section of this chapter. I also think that Sennett's ideas about cooperation are refreshingly different from much of the literature on collaborative and group work in schools.[20] I suggest that it is important to engage with these sub-skills of cooperation if we are to stand a chance of working together in communities to address the inequalities in our education system. As Sennett suggests, working cooperatively involves working with people who we may not understand, and working with people who we may not like.

Cooperation, professional development and leadership

Within this section of the chapter, I draw on research from the InterActive Education project,[21] which investigated the ways in which digital technologies could be used to transform learning in schools. One aspect of the project was to develop a model of professional development that involved teachers designing and evaluating new approaches for using digital technologies. The project was organised around what were called 'subject design teams' (in mathematics, English, history, geography, science, music and modern foreign languages). In this respect, the focus was on digital technologies being used to enhance subject knowledge learning, for example, learning about composition in music, learning about geometry or calculus in mathematics, learning about how to write in a foreign language. Each subject design team was made up of teachers and researchers, and the research on professional development was guided by the central question: how can teachers and researchers work together effectively to improve the quality of professional practice? We found that effective professional development requires a 'breaking out' of set roles and relationships in which researchers are traditionally seen as knowledge generators and teachers knowledge translators or users. For meaningful researcher–practitioner communities to emerge, the 'trading zones'[22] have to be places where 'co-learning' and the 'co-construction' of knowledge takes place. This moves beyond the idea of reciprocity, where roles are retained (the researcher being the active enquirer and the teacher the focus of the enquiry), to a position where both bring distinctiveness and complementarity to the knowledge-building process. The following extract from an interview with one of the partner-teachers illustrates this point:

> "People from an academic focus tend to look at things with a theoretical background. Teachers are always concerned with the practical. But we should be looking at teaching and learning more than we are able. The university partners are all teachers but each of you has a different perspective. It's been enjoyable – the different ways of working. It has made me think an awful lot … I think it's on my mind all the time." (Partner-teacher)

The capacity to engage in dialogue about implicit theories of teaching and learning and a willingness to problematise these with respect to particular knowledge domains were essential to the success of the experimentation with digital technologies that took place at the level of the classroom. Discussing research-warranted knowledge became an important part of the working relationship between teachers and researchers. At the outset, research findings were presented formally through 'raw' texts. This soon gave way to a more flexible approach based on appropriateness. At times, this meant sharing a research finding orally; at others, it meant being more complex and explaining ideas through more detailed discussion around a particular piece of evidence that had been chosen by the researchers on the request of the team. Here, more complex discussions led to open discussions, which often touched on methodology, theoretical perspectives and findings. What was important were the ways in which research-validated knowledge was opened up for discussion alongside other forms of knowledge that were more recognisable to the practitioner. This iterative approach also allowed research evidence to influence teachers' thinking as the teams and individuals examined new ideas in the light of well-established practices. The following comments from the interview data are characteristic:

> "Working closely with my university partner and the whole team was without doubt the biggest influence on my learning. I was introduced to new subject knowledge and new theories of teaching and learning. I was reading new things on language and research on language learning as well as discussing ideas." (Partner-teacher)

"Sometimes research was introduced but not in a pushy way, it was more thoughtful. The university people would try to explain why things had been done a particular way by using their own knowledge of the area and sometimes they would quote key sources and back them up with references. Then it would move to us choosing one for discussion at out next meeting." (Partner-teacher)

The process of design was conceived as an iterative process that involved the following phases:

- *deciding on a focused area of the curriculum* that students normally find difficult to learn and choosing digital technologies that could potentially enhance learning in this area;
- *out-of-the-classroom design as a thought experiment.* This involved developing activities and experimenting with the chosen digital technologies, while, at the same time, imagining how students would engage with these activities from the point of view of the intended learning. It also involved taking into account the background knowledge and experience of the students;
- *into-the-classroom contingent teaching*, which drew on the prepared activities while, at the same time, using and transforming what the students brought to the lesson in terms of out–of-school learning; and
- *out-of-the-classroom reflection* on and analysis of the design initiative using video data collected from the classroom experimentation.

In this approach, subject design initiatives usually started out as simple ideas that exploited the use of available technology in schools. Over time, and with iteration, they were transformed into powerful new uses of Information and Communications Technology (ICT) for learning. An important part of the process of professional development was the use of video data, which captured the processes of teaching and learning and were central to the analysis, interpretation and reflection phases of the design process.[23] The approach to professional development that emerged from the InterActive Education project involved developing practice-relevant knowledge within a network of teachers and researchers who worked together cooperatively, through the use of dialogue.

Whereas the focus within the InterActive Education project was on innovation using digital technologies, I suggest that the professional development model that emerged from the project could be used more generally. The approach would fit within the system put forward by

Mehta and discussed at the end of Chapter Seven, a system that moves away from centralised control of teachers and schools to networked groups of teachers taking responsibility for and evaluating their own practice. This is a system that involves academic researchers working cooperatively with teachers, which is very different from the current system in which educational academics are usually separated in their practice of research from teacher practitioners.

Within this approach, the use of digital video data as evidence and feedback on student learning and for capturing the relationship between teaching and learning is, in my opinion, potentially more valuable than the current focus in schools on performance data. The ongoing relationship between teachers and researchers and the focus on discussing the relationship between folk theories and evidence-informed theories were also key aspects of this particular professional development model.

In Chapter Two, I explained why I now think that I was naive in my earlier research because I believed that innovation and change could happen in a bottom-up way through working with teachers at the level of the classroom. Whereas I still believe that teachers are the main change agents in schools, and focusing on the level of the classroom is key to improving the quality of education, I now also understand the importance of the school head and the school leadership team in developing the culture of the school and creating a culture of what is possible at the level of the classroom.

Fullan draws attention to the importance of culture as opposed to structures, pointing out that 're-culturing is the name of the game':

> We tend to meet any situation by reorganizing. What a wonderful method this can be for creating the illusion of progress: while producing confusion, inefficiency and demoralization. Structure does make a difference, but it is not the main point of achieving success. Transforming the culture – changing the way we do things around here – is the main point. I call this re-culturing. Leading in a culture of change means creating a culture (not just a structure) of change. It does not mean adopting innovations, one after another; it does mean producing the capacity to seek, critically assess, and selectively incorporate new ideas and practices – all the time, inside the organization as well as outside it.[24]

Fullan emphasises that there can never be a recipe book or a checklist for change because change is not a step-by-step process. He points out that school leaders are 'vulnerable to seeking the comforting clarity of off-the-shelf solutions', [25] they can feel under pressure to change. Moreover, school effectiveness is driven by a Total Quality Management (TQM) approach to leadership, which involves working backwards from a goal and knowing what you need to achieve. Fullan argues that change in complex situations such as classrooms is a process that cannot be understood simply in terms of cause and effect, and involves working forwards into the unknown in a more emergent way. [26]

In emphasising teachers as change agents, I am not advocating a frenetic approach to change. However, I am suggesting that teachers should find ways of examining their practice and, in particular, the relationship between their teaching and student learning while, at the same time, taking into account theoretical and evidence-informed knowledge. This is a risky business and I suggest that teachers should work together cooperatively in professional development communities to support each other in a process of experimentation and critical reflection. I am also suggesting that academic researchers have a role to play within such professional development communities, but that for meaningful researcher–practitioner communities to emerge, the meeting between teachers and researchers has to enable 'co-learning' and the 'co-construction' of knowledge to take place. However, for professional development practices to happen, school leaders have to value professional development, supporting teachers to participate in professional development communities.

Schooling and social justice

Throughout this book, I have argued for the continued importance of schooling within what is called a digital age, that is, an age in which digital artefacts are ubiquitous, from smart phones, to global positioning systems, to online social networks. Within this digital age, there are many people who situate themselves in what could be called the 'digital futures' camp, and these people suggest that schools are becoming redundant within society. By contrast, there are others who are in what could be called the 'school improvement' camp, and these people place an emphasis on raising educational standards. In general, those in the latter camp have not critically engaged with the potential of the digital, and those in the digital futures camp do not adequately take into account issues of social justice. For example, at the time of writing this book, there is considerable hype around the potential of massive open online courses (moocs) to open up educational opportunities to those from disadvantaged backgrounds. However, emerging research is beginning to show that 'underachieving, minority and disadvantaged students fared particularly badly when they took online classes. The promise of moocs to improve access and democratise knowledge is a chimera'.[27] In this respect, digital technologies can exacerbate inequalities and so a much more critical approach has to be taken with respect to the relationship between digital technologies and social justice.

In general, those who herald the digital as a means of providing access to education to disadvantaged communities believe that knowledge can be readily accessed from the Internet, or from listening to a lecturer at a distance. They do not take into account what Olson calls the difference between personal beliefs and knowledge with a capital K, or what Vygotsky calls the difference between everyday and academic knowledge. They do not take into account the challenges of the fourth and future pedagogy discussed in Chapter Seven, in which teacher and students first have to negotiate joint intentions before the process of engaging with new Knowledge worlds can begin.

In Chapter Five, I introduced Young and Muller's scenarios for future education, and argued that it is Future 3 scenario that should be a model for education in the 21st century. Here, the conceptual challenges of learning subject knowledge are recognised and knowledge is considered socially constructed, but that some forms of knowledge are more powerful than others. In adopting Future 3 scenario, the challenges of teaching students powerful knowledge that is qualitatively different from their everyday knowledge should not be underestimated. Such knowledge cannot be taught through rules and rote, and Olson's fourth pedagogy discussed in Chapter Seven points to a way forward. However, teachers and researchers working within each school knowledge domain (eg English, music, history, mathematics) need to carry out research at the level of the classroom in order to move the theorising about this fourth pedagogy forward. And, as the French understand well with their concept of Didactiques des Mathématiques,[28] issues of pedagogy cannot be separated from the knowledge that is being learned.[29]

Whereas what happens at the level of the classroom is a key aspect of developing a quality education system, the deep divisions within the educational system have to be tackled at a more structural level. Throughout this book, I have argued that the English educational system is doubly divided: first, it is divided into fee-charging private schools and state-maintained schools; and, second, the state-maintained schools are also divided into those that provide a good quality education for their students and those that do not (estimated as being approximately a quarter of state-maintained schools in England). In other words, from a capabilities perspective, a quarter of state-maintained schools do not provide young people with the opportunities to choose a wide range of university and employment options when they leave school. Both divisions need to be tackled, and Andrew Adonis has recently put forward creative suggestions for overcoming the private–state school divide. First, he suggests that 'Every successful private school, and private school foundation, should sponsor at least one academy, true to its charitable mission and leveraging its success and its networks within the state-funded and fee-paying sectors'.[30] Second, he suggests that:

> Successful private day schools should be enabled and encouraged to join the state sector as academies, on the model of the first wave of 'direct grant' academies since 2000. On this model the private school becomes an academy, retaining its independent management and character but without fees. It exchanges academically selective admissions for all-ability admissions, but with a large catchment area and 'banded' admissions to ensure a full comprehensive ability range. It also continues with a large sixth form, underpinning continued very strong academic performance.[31]

Interestingly, two previously fee-charging private schools in Bristol have converted to become state-maintained academies, and although some people are critical of these changes, the overall impact in terms of educational opportunities available for young people in Bristol has to be positive.

I have always struggled with the idea of private education in the UK, and the way in which it divides people. When my son started to study medicine at university in the early 1990s, the vast majority of his fellow students had been educated at private fee-charging schools. When they learned that he had obtained very good A level results from a state-maintained comprehensive school,[32] they were often incredulous. From their privileged and elite private school background, they did not know that it was possible to excel educationally from a state school. It was completely outside their realm of experience. Recently, my son has returned to the university where he studied medicine to complete his training as a surgeon. None of the surgeons who he works with send their children to state schools, and he finds that he often has to defend his decision to send his own children to a state primary school. What can this mean for children from state schools who apply to study medicine at elite universities? I find it depressing that such a divided situation continues to exist within the UK in the 21st century, a situation where a privileged elite that represents 7% of the population has so little engagement with 93% of the population that they cannot respect and understand the value of an education from a state school.

I argue that something urgently has to be done about our divided educational system and it is interesting to imagine what would happen to the educational opportunities for all young people in the city of Bristol if Adonis's manifesto for change were adopted, and the fee-charging private schools began a process of working cooperatively with the state-maintained schools in the city. However, it is important to note that all of the fee-charging schools are in the north of the City and so such a development would not change the North–South divide in Bristol in terms of educational opportunities available for young people. A change would be needed to the admissions policy of schools because, apart from a few exceptions, these currently stipulate 'distance from the school' as the most important criterion for admission. My mother travelled 13 miles by bus from the village of Dersingham to her secondary school in Kings Lynn. I travelled eight miles by bus from Raglan to my secondary school in Monmouth and my daughter travelled five miles by bus from Harpenden to her secondary school in St Albans. From a social justice perspective, it is difficult to imagine how the state-maintained educational system within Bristol can improve without bus travel becoming economically and logistically viable.

Endnote: on the pleasure of making and writing

At 15, I had no idea what job I wanted to do, no idea of a career path. I knew that I loved mathematics and so choosing to study mathematics at university was an obvious choice. After this, I worked for a while as a computer programmer, and then as a university research assistant. I then spent time living in the US, became a full-time mother for several years, before returning to work as a teacher, first in a school and then in a further education college, teaching computer programming, mathematics and statistics.[33] But I was always interested in the idea of research. My father had worked on his PhD at home when I was a young girl, carrying out experiments on ultrasound in what looked like a fish tank set up in a bedroom of our house. I have no real memory of his work apart from a visual image of the experimental set-up, but I imagine this had an impact on me as a young girl between the ages of five and nine. I also experienced my husband doing research for his doctorate in mechanical engineering when we were first married. So the idea of research was not a mystery to me and in the back of my mind was the thought that one day it would be my turn to become a researcher.

My career as an academic did not start until I was in my late 30s, and I have spent the last 30 years learning the craft of writing. The highly specialist educational system that was dominant in England in the 1950s and 1960s meant that I had not studied or practised writing since the age of 16. For A levels, I specialised in physics and mathematics, and at university, I studied mathematics (with a little computer programming as part of a course on numerical analysis). As an apprentice academic and when studying for my doctoral degree, I began to realise that I very much enjoyed writing. It turned out that 'writing' was just about part of my capability set, and I can now appreciate what I learned about the practice of writing at my grammar school in the 1950s. I can now see how five years of relentlessly practising essay-writing and five years of practising the craft of the précis was good-enough preparation for my career as an academic. But without such a focus on writing in my pre-16 school courses, I may not have had the freedom to choose to become an academic in later life.

I have chosen to use the phrase 'the craft of writing', and I see similarities between the craft of writing and the craft of sewing. I learned to sew from my mother and when younger, made all of my own clothes. I learned how to make dress patterns by attending an evening class and for a while in my 20s, designed my clothes. Then, I would cut out the pieces, pin them together and try on the garment to get a sense of the whole, what it might look like when it was finished. I do something similar when writing. I assemble ideas in rough text, put them into some sort of order, and only later work on the detailed crafting of the sentences. Some people find this approach difficult when we work collaboratively together. But in not finishing my ideas until the end, I hope that I leave open a space for dialogue and cooperation. When writing collaboratively with someone who sends me a piece of 'finished' text, I find it very difficult to know where and how to contribute with my own ideas, how we can start the dialogic process of writing together.

In writing this book I have chosen to weave pictures and images throughout the text. Why have I done this? I know I was influenced by the work of Sebald and am fascinated by the way he inserts images into his text without explaining what they are.[34] But my purpose relates more to a desire to weave the personal into the academic, because of a belief that who we become relates to the opportunities we have in life and that these relate to the people with whom we have lived, the teachers we have engaged with, the technologies we have used and the institutions we have been a part of. I also believe that the personal influences our informal beliefs and that through coming to understand the personal, we can challenge our own values, our own folk theories, which is an important part of developing more robust academic theory. Another reason for including images in this work is that the visual is important to me and, nowadays, when producing digital text, it is possible to experiment with interspersing images into a written text and possible to experiment with meanings associated with the relationship between text and images.

This book is dedicated to my family and, in particular, my mother, Joan Hatfield, who died aged 93 on 12 March 2013. For much of the last few months of her life, I was struggling with writing this book, as well as struggling with the idea of very old age. My mother grew up in a poor rural Norfolk family, but she was given the opportunity of a good secondary school education, and in her own words:

> "At the age of 10, I passed an examination and went to King's Lynn High School. I travelled each day by bus. Because we were poor, Norfolk gave me a grant to pay for my clothes and because dad had served in the war, the British Legion paid for my lunches. I was very happy at school and always tried to do well."

Her school education provided her with the capabilities to choose a university education, and her university education enabled her to become a geography teacher. That she chose to become a full-time mother for many years and worked as a teacher for a relatively short part of her long life was her choice, and was normal for women at that time. This is very different for my daughter, who chooses to practise as a full-time architect at the same time as being a mother. In her later life, my mother said that she would have liked to have become an artist, but that this had not been a possibility for a young girl from a poor family in the 1930s. This possibility could not have been imagined by her, her teachers or her family. But, in some ways, in leading the life she chose, my mother opened up the possibility for my daughter to become an architect. As Joanna said at her grandmother's funeral:

> "One doesn't always recognise how remarkable those that are close to you are, and years ago, when I was an 18-year-old au-pair in Chicago, I met up with Adeline Stanley, an old university friend of Grandma's. She asked whether I'd realised it was so special to be third-generation educated, and how unusual it was to have a grandmother that went to university. Now, more than 20 years later, I understand much more about how remarkable Grandma's life was, and also how hard it would have been.[35]
>
> One legacy that she leaves with us is her creativity. When people ask about the rings on my fingers, I say they were made by my grandmother, then when they inevitably ask, 'Was she a jeweller?', I say 'No, these are just some of the things grandma made in her life' and I feel so proud of that. I love to be surrounded by the things she has made, the pottery, the dresses, the cushions, and I recognise that my own love of making and an eye for composition, albeit in buildings, comes from her."

Whereas it is difficult for me to imagine the education of my as-yet-unborn great-grandchildren, the education of my mother's great-grandchildren is already happening. And as I watch them start school, I know that it cannot be right that some people can choose to live in areas where a good education is a possibility while others have no choice about the quality of education on offer to their children.

The capabilities approach argues for the importance of experimenting with practical changes on the ground, and monitoring whether such practical steps are reducing or exacerbating social and educational divides. For me, this means working as a governor of a South Bristol school, working to raise the quality of education available to young people in South

Bristol. This transcends any views I might have about whether or not Academies should be replacing local authority schools, any views I might have about educational policies that are being promoted by the political party currently in power.

Finishing and ending this book has been difficult, as is the finishing and ending of a life. For me, there are always new ideas that I am thinking and reading about. But without a self-imposed deadline, there may be no ending. Whereas finishing is difficult, there is also a huge pleasure in putting the finishing touches on a work, as there is pleasure in celebrating a life lived. In the last third of my own life, I hope to return to some of the craft work that was important to me when I was younger, and now that this book is finished, there will be the space to pursue this ambition, the space to turn my imaginings into reality.

Notes

[1] This school has now substantially reduced the vocational courses on offer in the pre-16 phase of education.

[2] Wolf (2011, p 81).

[3] Sutherland et al (2008).

[4] Sen (2009).

[5] Walker and Unterhalter (2007, p 5).

[6] Walker and Unterhalter (2007, p 5).

[7] Sen (2009, p 106).

[8] Sen (2009, p 106).

[9] Sen (2009, p 5).

[10] Sennet (2009, p 140).

[11] Sennet (2009, p 141).

[12] Sennet (2009, p 142).

[13] Nussbaum and Sen (1993).

[14] Bakhtin (1981).

[15] Bakhtin (1981, p 19).

[16] Sennett (2009, p 23).

[17] Sennett (2012, p 122).

[18] Sennett (2009, p 21).

[19.] I first came across the work of Bakhtin through my reading of Wertsch (1991).

[20.] See, for example, Blatchford et al (2006).

[21.] See Sutherland et al (2008).

[22.] Galison (1997).

[23.] See for example Jewitt (2012).

[24.] Fullan (2001, p 44)

[25.] Fullan (2001, p 45).

[26.] For further discussion of complexity and education see Davis and Sumara (2006).

[27.] Vernon (2013).

[28.] Brousseau and Balacheff (1997).

[29.] To a certain extent, many researchers within mathematics education also understand this issue. See, for example, Brown and Coles (2012).

[30] Adonis (2012, p 256).

[31.] Adonis (2012, p 256).

[32.] Verulam School, St Albans.

[33.] Further Education Colleges in England offer both vocational and academic courses for young people in the post 16 phase of education, although they tend to focus on vocational courses.

[34.] See: http://observatory.designobserver.com/entry.html?entry=23618

[35.] My grandmother, Ella Mary Martha Reynolds, took her own life on 6 June 1938, when my mother was in her first year of university. Her younger brother, Barrie Reynolds, wrote the following for my mother's funeral on 5 April 2013, speaking about the incident for almost the first time:

> "We lived in a basic one-room-up and one-room-down house with a single storey room to one side, which was used as a kitchen, with no running water or drainage system. Our lack of an on-tap water supply meant that we used rainwater taken from a large tank outside the back door for washing ourselves first thing in the morning. So, in winter time, we had to break the ice before scooping water out of the tank and using it in an outdoor scullery. Our main wash when quite young was in a galvanised bath in front of the open fire in the living room. Initially, Joan and Mary shared a space for a bed at the top of the stairs

whilst Derek and I shared a bed in the same room as our parents, and Jack, with TB [tuberculosis] of the spine, slept in a wooden structure, open at one side apart from canvas curtains, on a rotatable base in the yard outside. Our water supply situation played a sinister part in our lives. When Joan was at QMC in 1938 and I was nine-and-a-bit years old, our mother, no doubt suffering from problems including the menopause, took her own life by drowning in the well in the yard outside, where Mary found her."

References

21st Century Schools (2004) 'A joint initiative between CABE and RIBA'. Available at: www.buildingfutures.org.uk

Academies Commission (2013) *Unleashing greatness: getting the best from an academised system*, London: Pearson Think Tank/RSA.

Adonis A (2012) *Education, education, education, reforming England's schools, Birkbeck schools*, London: Biteback Publishing.

Alexander, R. and Armstrong, M. (2010) *Children, their world, their education: Final report and recommendations of the Cambridge Primary Review*, London and New York, NY: Taylor & Francis.

Armstrong, V., Barnes, S., Sutherland, R., Curran, S., Mills, S. and Thompson, I. (2005) 'Collaborative research methodology for investigating teaching and learning: the use of interactive whiteboard technology', *Educational Review*, 57(4): 457–469.

Bakhtin M.M. (1981) *The dialogic imagination: four essays by M.M. Bakhtin*, Michael Holquist ed, Caryl Emerson and Michael Holquist trans, Austin, TX: University of Texas Press.

Ball, S.J. (2008) *The education debate*, Bristol: The Policy Press.

Barrett, P., Zhang, Z., Moffat, J. and Kobbacy, K. (2013) 'A holistic, multi-level analysis identifying the impact of classroom design on pupils' learning', *Building and Environment*, 59 (January): 678–689.

Benn, M. (2011) *School wars. The battle for Britain's education*, London and New York: Verso.

Bentley, T. and Miller, R. (2006) 'Personalisation: Getting the questions right', in *OECD Schooling for Tomorrow. Personalising Education*, Paris: Organisation for Economic Co-operation and Development Publications, pp 115-125.

Bereiter, C. (2002) *Education and mind in the knowledge age*, Mahwah, NJ: Lawrence Erlbaum.

Bernstein, B. (1990) *The structuring of pedagogic discourse: vol IV class codes and control*, London and New York, NY: Routledge.

Bernstein, B. (2000) *Pedagogy, symbolic control and identity: Theory research and critique* (2nd edn), Oxford: Rowman and Littlefield.

Birmingham (2009) 'BSF education design toolkit volume 1 induction document', Catlyst.

Blatchford, P., Baines, E., Rubie-Davies, C., Bassett, P. and Chowne, A. (2006) 'The effect of a new approach to group work on pupil–pupil and teacher–pupil interactions', *Journal of Educational Psychology*, 98(4): 750–65.

Boli, J. and Ramirez, F. (1992) 'Compulsory schooling in the Western contemporary context, in F. Arnove, P. Geoffrey and G. Kelly (eds) *Emergent issues in education, comparative perspectives*, Albany, NY: State University of New York Press.

Bowles, S. and Gintis, H. (1976) *Schooling in capitalist America, educational reform and the contradictions of economic life*, London: Routledge.

Broadfoot, P., Timmis, S. and Sutherland, R. (2013) *Ethical issues in technology enhanced assessment*, available at: www.bris.ac.uk/education/research/sites/tea/publications/index.html

Brousseau, G. and Balacheff, N. (1997) *Theory of didactical situations in mathematics: Didactique des mathématiques, 1970–1990*, translated by M. Cooper, R. Sutherland and V. Warfield, Dordrecht: Kluwer academic publishers.

Brown, L. and Coles, A. (2012) 'Developing "deliberate analysis" for learning mathematics and for mathematics teacher education: how the enactive approach to cognition frames reflection', *Educational Studies in Mathematics*, 80: 217–31.

Burgess, S., Wilson, D. and Worth, J. (2010) 'A natural experiment in school accountability: the impact of school performance information on pupil progress and sorting', Centre for Market and Public Policy Organisation, University of Bristol, working paper No 10/246.

Butterfield, A., Sutherland, R. and Molyneux-Hodgson, S. (2000) 'Learning conversions in science: the case of vocational students in the UK', *Association for Learning Technology Journal*, 8(3): 89–104.

Claxton, G. (2002) *Building learning power*, Bristol: TLO Limited.

Claxton, G., Chambers, M., Powell, G. and Lucas, B. (2011) *The learning powered school. Pioneering 21st century education*, Bristol: ITO Ltd.

Clifton, J. and Cook, W. (2012) 'A long division: closing the attainment gap in England's schools', report for IPPR.

Coffield, F. and Williamson, B. (2011) *From exam factories to communities of discovery. The democratic route*, London: Institute of Education, University of London.

Cole, M. and Engeström, Y. (1993) 'A cultural-historical approach to distributed cognition', in G. Salomon (ed) *Distributed cognition*, Cambridge: CUP.

Davis, B. and Sumara, D. (2006) *Complexity and education. Inquiries into learning, teaching, and research*, New York, NY and London: LEA, Taylor and Francis Group.

Davis, B., Dennis, S. and Luce-Kapler, R. (2000) *Engaging minds: learning and teaching in a complex world*, London: Lawrence Erlbaum Publishers.

Davydov, V.V. (1990) 'Types of generalization in instruction: logical and psychological problems in the structuring of school curricula. Soviet studies in mathematics education. Volume 2', National Council of Teachers of Mathematics, 1906 Association Dr., Reston, VA 22091.

Design Commission (2011) *Restarting Britain: design education and growth*, London: Policy Connect.

DfES (Department for Education and Skills) (2006) '2020 vision', report of the Teaching and Learning in 2020 Review Group.

DfES (2009) 'Twelve outstanding secondary schools: exceeding against the odds', Ofsted report.

Dobson, T. and John Willinsky (2009) 'Digital literacy', in D. Olson and N. Torrance (eds) *Cambridge handbook on literacy*, Cambridge: Cambridge University Press.

Dorling, D. (2010) *Injustice. Why social inequality persists*, Bristol: The Policy Press.

Durkin, K. and Shire, B. (eds) (1991) *Language in mathematical education: research and practice*, Buckingham: Open University Press.

Dweck, C. (2012) *Mindset: how you can fulfil your potential*, New York, NY: Balantine Books.

Eagle, S. (2012) 'Learning in the early years: social interactions around picturebooks, puzzles and digital technologies', *Computers and Education*, 59(1): 38–49.

Eagle, S. and Sutherland, R. (2012) *Future Brunel report*, Internal Report, Bristol: University of Bristol.

Eagle, S., Manches, A., O'Malley, C., Plowman, L. and Sutherland, R. (2008) *From research to design: perspectives on early years, digital technologies and numeracy*, Bristol: Futurelab.

Engeström, Y. (1999) 'Activity theory and individual and social transformation', *Perspectives on activity theory*, pp 19–38.

Engeström, Y. and Sannino, A. (2010) 'Studies of expansive learning: foundations, findings and future challenges', *Educational Research Review*, 5(1): 1–24.

Facer, K. (2011) *Learning futures: education, technology and social change*, London and New York, NY: Routledge.

Facer, K., Furlong, J., Furlong, R. and Sutherland, R. (2003) *Screenplay: children and computing in the home*, London and New York, NY: Routledge Falmer.

Fischer, F., Wild, W., Zirn, L. and Sutherland, R. (2013) *Grand challenge problems in technology enhanced learning*, New York: Springer-Verlag.

Fullan, M. (2001) *Leading in a culture of change*, San Francisco, CA: Jossey-Bass, John Wiley and Sons.

Fullan, M. (2012) 'Understanding change', in *The Jossey-Bass reader on educational leadership*, San Francisco, CA: Jossey-Bass Publishers.

Furber, S. (2012) *Shut down or restart? The way forward for computing in UK schools*, London: The Royal Society.

Furlong, J. (2013) 'Globalisation, neoliberalism, and the reform of teacher education in England'. *The Educational Forum*, 77(1): 28–50.

Furlong, J. and Davies, C. (2012) 'Young people, new technologies and learning at home: taking context seriously', *Oxford Review of Education*, 38(1): 45–62.

Galison, P. (1997) *Image & logic: A material culture of microphysics*, Chicago, IL: The University of Chicago Press.

Gall, M. and Breeze, N. (2005) 'Music composition lessons: the multimodal affordances of technology', *Educational Review*, 57(4): 415–33.

Gall, M., Lazarus, E., Tidmarsh, C. and Breeze, N. (2009) Creative Designs for Learning, in R. Sutherland et al (2008).

Gee, J.P. (2003) 'What video games have to teach us about learning and literacy', *Computers in Entertainment (CIE)*, 1(1): 20.

Gee, J.P. (2009) 'Deep learning properties of good digital games: How far can they go', in U. Ritterfeld, M. Cody and P. Vorderer (eds), *Serious games: Mechanisms and effects*, 67–82, Abingdon: Routledge.

Gibson, J.J. (1977) 'The theory of affordances', in R. Shaw and J. Bransford (eds) *Perceiving, acting and knowing: Toward an ecological psychology*, Hillsdale, NJ: Lawrence Erlbaum, pp 67–82.

Goodman, A., Gregg, G. and Washbrook, E. (2010) 'Children's educational attainment and the aspirations, attitudes and behaviours of parents and children through childhood in the UK', *Longitudinal and Life Course Studies*, 2(1): 1–18.

Greevy, H., Knox, A., Nunney, F., and Pye, J. (2012) *The effects of the English Baccalaureate*, Department for Education Research Report DFE – RR249R, London: DfE.

Haenen, J., Schrijnemakers, H. and Stufkens, J. (2003) 'Sociocultural theory and the practice of teaching historical concepts', in A. Kozulin, B. Gindis, S. Miller & V. Ageyev (eds), *Vygotsky's educational theory in cultural context*, New York: Cambridge Univerity Press.

Harris, P. (2012) *Trusting what you're told: how children learn from others*, Cambridge, MA: The Belknap Press of Harvard University Press.

Harwood, E. (2010) *England's schools. History, architecture and adaption*, Swindon: English Heritage.

Hattie, J. (2009) *Visible learning: a synthesis of over 800 meta-analyses relating to achievement*, Abingdon: Routledge.

Herlihy, D.V. (2004) *Bicycle: the history*, Yale University Press.

Higgins, S. (2003) 'Does ICT improve teaching and learning in schools?', A BERA Professional User Review. Available at: http://learning.wales.gov.uk/docs/learningwales/publications/121122ictlearningen.pdf

Higgins, S., Katsipataki, M., Kokotsaki, D., Coleman, R., Major, L.E. and Coe, R. (2013) *The Sutton Trust–Education Endowment Foundation teaching and learning toolkit*, London: Education Endowment Foundation.

Holloway, S. and Valentine, G. (2001) '"It's only as stupid as you are": children's and adults' negotiation of ICT competence at home and at school', *Social & Cultural Geography*, 2(1): 25–42.

Hopkins, D. (2006) 'Introduction', in *OECD Schooling for Tomorrow. Personalising Education*, Paris: Organisation for Eceonomic Co-Operation and Development Publications, pp 17–20.

Howsam, L., Stray, C., Jenkins, A., Secord, J. A., Vaninskaya, A. and Howsam, L. (2007) 'What the Victorians learned: perspectives on nineteenth-century schoolbooks', *Journal of Victorian Culture*, 12(2): 262–85.

Hoyles, C. and Lagrange, J.B. (eds) (2010) *Mathematics education and technology-rethinking the terrain*, New York: Springer.

Hoyles, C. and Noss, R. (eds) (1992) *Logo and mathematics: research and curriculum issues*, Cambridge, MA: MIT press.

Hoyles, C. and Sutherland, R. (1989) *Logo mathematics in the classroom*, London: Routledge.

Jenkins, H. (2009) *Confronting the challenges of participatory culture: media education for the 21st century*, Cambridge, MA: MIT Press.

Jewitt, C. (2012) *An introduction to using video for research*, National Centre for Research Methods, Working Paper 03/12, available at: http://eprints.ncrm.ac.uk/2259/4/NCRM_workingpaper_0312.pdf

JMC (Joint Mathematical Council) (2011) 'Technologies and mathematics education', report for the Joint Mathematical Council of the UK.

Jones, I. and Alcock, L. (2012) 'Using adaptive comparative judgement to assess mathematics'. Available at: http://education.lms.ac.uk/2012/06/using-adaptive-comparative-judgement-to-assess-mathematics/

Karpov, Y.V. (2003) 'Vygotsky's doctrine of scientific concepts. Its role for contemporary education', in A. Kozulin, B. Gindis, V.S. Ageyev and S.M. Miller (eds) *Vygotsky's educational theory in cultural context*, Cambridge: Cambridge University Press, pp 65–82.

Kutz, M. (2001) 'Situating practices: the archive and the filing cabinet', *Historical Geography*, 2: 26–37. Available at: http://historical-geography.net/volume_29_2001/kurtz.pdf

Leadbeater, C. (2005) *The shape of things to come: personalised learning through collaboration*, London: DfES.

Leadbeater, C. (2006) 'The future of public services: personalised learning', in OECD (ed) *Personalising education*, Paris: OECD Publishing.

Mansell, W. (2007) *Education by numbers: the tyranny of testing*, London: Politico's.

Marshall, P. (ed) (2013) *The tail, how England's schools fail one child in five – and what can be done*, London: Profile Books.

Maton, K. and Moore, R. (eds) (2010) *Social realism, knowledge and the sociology of education, coalitions of the mind*, London: Continuum International Publishing Group.

Matthewman, S. (2009) 'Discerning Literacy', Chapter 6 in R. Sutherland, S. Robertson and P. John, *Improving classroom learning with ICT*, Abingdon: Routledge.

Mehta, J. (2013) *The allure of order: high hopes, dashed expectations, and the troubled quest to remake American schooling*, Oxford: Oxford University Press.

Miliband, D. (2006) 'Choice and voice in personalised learning', in *Personalising education*, Paris: OECD Publishing, 21–30.

Miller, R. (2011) *Vygotsky in perspective*, Cambridge: Cambridge University Press.

Monbiot, G. (2013) 'When the rich are born to rule, the results can be fatal', *The Guardian*, 29 January.

Moore, R. and Young, M. (2010) 'Reconceptualising knowledge and the curriculum in the sociology of education', in K. Maton and R. Moore (eds) *Social realism, knowledge and the sociology of education, coalitions of the mind*, London: Continuum International Publishing Group.

Morgan, J. (2011) 'Enquiring Minds: a radical curriculum project?', *Forum*, Vol 53(2): 261–272.

Morgan, J. and Williamson, B. (2008) *Enquiring minds: schools, knowledge and educational change*, Bristol: Futurelab (open access licence available at: www.futurelab.org.uk/policies).

Morris, E. (2013) 'Time for royal college of teaching', *The Guardian*, 22 April. Available at: www.guardian.co.uk/education/2013/apr/22/royal-college-of-teaching-establish

Moses, R. (2001) *Radical equations: maths, literacy and civil rights*, Boston, MA: Beacon Press.

National Audit office (2009) *The Building Schools of the Future Programme, renewing the secondary school estate*, London: Stationary Office. Available at: www.nao.org.uk/wp-content/uploads/2009/02/0809135.pdf

National College for School Leadership (NCSL) (2012) The growth of academy chains: Implications for leaders and leadership, available at: http://dera.ioe.ac.uk/14536/

Noss, R. (1983) 'Starting LOGO: interim report of the Chiltern LOGO Project', Advisory Unit for Computer Based Education, Hatfield.

Nunes, T., Schliemann, A.D. and Carraher, D.W. (1993) *Street mathematics and school mathematics*, Cambridge: Cambridge University Press.

Nussbaum, N. and Sen, A. (1993) *The quality of life*, Oxford: Clarendon Press.

Olivero, F., Sutherland, R. and John, P. (2009) 'Learning and technology', Chapter 3 in R. Sutherland, S. Robertson and P. John (eds) *Improving classroom learning with ICT*, Abingdon: Routledge.

Olson, D.R. (1994) *The world on paper. The conceptual and cognitive implications of writing and reading*, Cambridge: Cambridge University Press.

Olson, D.R. (2003) *Psychological theory and educational reform. How school remakes mind and society*, Cambridge: Cambridge University Press.

Olson, D.R. (2012) 'Agency and intentionality in pedagogy: where the accountability train left the tracks'. Available at: www.learningcultures. net/journal/archive/agency-and-intentionality-in-pedagogy-where-the-accountability-train-left-the-tracks

Olson, D.R. and Bruner, J.S. (1996) 'Folk psychology and folk pedagogy', *The Handbook of Education and Human Development*, Edited by D. Olson and N. Torrance, Malden, MA: Blackwell Publishers.

Panofsky, C. (2003) 'The relations of learning and student social class: towards re-"socializing" sociocultural learning theory', in A. Kozulin, B. Gindis, V. Ageyev and S. Miller (eds) *Vygotsky's educational theory in cultural context*, Cambridge: Cambridge University Press.

Papert, S. (1980) *Mindstorms: children, computers, and powerful ideas*, New York, NY: Basic Books.

Papert, S. (1993) *The children's machine: Rethinking school in the age of the computer*, New York, NY: Basic Books.

Pea, R. (1985) 'Beyond amplification: using the computer to reorganise mental functioning', *r*, 20(4): 167–82.

Pea, R. (1993) 'Practices of distributed intelligence and designs for education', in G. Salomon (ed) *Distributed cognition*, Cambridge: CUP.

Perkins, D.N. (1993) 'Person-plus: a distributed view of thinking and learning', in G. Salomon (ed) *Distributed cognitions: psychological and educational considerations*, Cambridge: Cambridge University Press, pp 88–110.

Places for Learning, Fielden Clegg Bradley Studios, available at: www. fcbstudios.com/pdfs/Schools.FINAL.pdf

Pring, R. (2010). 'The need for a wider vision of learning. International Studies', *Sociology of Education*, 20(1): 83–91.

Pring, R. (2013) *The life and death of secondary education for all*, London and New York, NY: Routledge.

Raphael Reed, L., Croudace, C., Baxter, A., Last, K. & Harrison, N. (2007) *Young participation in higher education: A sociocultural study of educational engagement in Bristol South Parliamentary Constituency*, Project Report, Bristol: UWE on behalf of HEFCE.

Rasbash, J., Leckie, G., Pillinger, R. and Jenkins, J. (2010) 'Children's educational progress: partitioning family, school and area effects', *Journal of the Royal Statistical Society*, 173(3): 657–82.

Rata, E. (2012) 'The politics of knowledge in education', *British Educational Research Journal*, 38(1): 103–124.

Royal Society (2012) 'Computing in schools: shut down or restart', report for The Royal Society.

Royal Society/JMC Working Group (1997) Teaching and learning algebra pre-19, http://royalsociety.org/uploadedFiles/Royal_Society_Content/ policy/publications/1997/10183.pdf

Salomon, G. (1990) Cognitive effects with and of computer technology, *Communication research*, 17(1): 26–44.

Sanger, J. (2001) 'The demise of UK schooling and the rise of the individual learner', in A. Loveless and V. Ellis (eds) *ICT, pedagogy and the curriculum, subject to change*, London: Routledge.

Schmittau, J. (2003) 'Cultural-historical theory and mathematics education', in A. Kozulin, B. Gindis, S. Miller & V. Ageyev (eds), *Vygotsky's educational theory in cultural context*, New York: Cambridge Univerity Press, pp 225–245.

Seaborne, M.V.J. and Lowe, R. (1977) *The English school: its architecture and organization. Vol. 2, 1870–1970*, Reading: Routledge & Kegan Paul.

Sebha, J. and Brittain, G. (2007) 'An investigation of personalised learning approaches used by schools', Research Report RR843, Department for Education and Skills.

Selwyn, N. (2011) *Schools and schooling in the digital age: a critical analysis*, London and New York, NY: Routledge.

Sen, A. (1993) 'Capability and well-being,' *The quality of life*, 1(9): 30–54.

Sen, A. (1999) *Development as freedom*, Oxford: Oxford University Press.

Sen, A. (2001) *Inequality reexamined*, New York, NY: Russell Sage Foundation.

Sen, A. (2008) 'The economics of happiness and capability', in L. Bruni, F. Comin and M. Pugno (eds) *Capabilities and happiness,* Oxford: Oxford University Press.

Sen, A. (2009) *The idea of justice*, London: Allen Lane, Penguin Books.

Sennett, R. (2008) *The craftsman*, London: Penguin Books.

Sennett, R. (2012) *Together, the rituals, pleasures & politics of cooperation*, London: Penguin Books.

Somekh, B. and Davis, N. (eds) (1997) *Using inoformation technology effectively in teaching and learning*, London: Routledge.

Somekh, B., Lewin, C., Mavers, D., Fisher, T., Harrison, C., Haw, K. and Scrimshaw, P. (2002) *ImpaCT2: pupils' and teachers' perceptions of ICT in the home, school and community*, British Educational Communications and Technology Agency (BECTA).

Steiner, J.V. and Mahn, H. (1996) 'Sociocultural approaches to learning and development: a Vygoskian framework', *Educational Psychologist*, 31(3/4): 191–206.

Sutherland, R. (1989) 'Providing a computer-based framework for algebraic thinking', *Educational Studies in Mathematics*, 20(3): 317–44.

Sutherland, R. (1992) 'What is algebraic about programming in Logo?', in C. Hoyles and R. Noss (eds) *Logo and mathematics: research and curriculum issues*, Cambridge, MA: MIT press, pp 37–54.

Sutherland, R. (2007) *Teaching for learning mathematics*, London: McGraw-Hill International.

Sutherland, R. and Rojano, T. (1993) 'A spreadsheet approach to solving algebra problems', *Journal of Mathematical Behaviour*, 12(4): 351–83.

Sutherland, R.J. and Sutherland, J. (2010) 'Space, learning and technology', in K. Makitalo-Siegl, F. Kaplan, J. Zottmann and F. Fischer (ed) *Classroom of the future: orchestrating collaborative spaces*, Rotterdam: Sense Publishers.

Sutherland, R., Howell, D. and Wolf, A. (1996) *A spreadsheet approach to maths for GNVQ engineering*, London, Sydney and Auckland: Arnold, Hodder Headline.

Sutherland, R., Robertson, S. and John, P. (2008) *Improving classroom learning with ICT*, London: Routledge.

Sutherland, R., Yee, W.C., McNess, E. and Harris, R. (2010) 'Supporting learning in the transition from primary to secondary school'. Available at: www.bris.ac.uk/cmpo/publications/other/transition.pdf

Sutton Trust (2010) 'Responding to the new landscape for university access', December, The Sutton Trust.

Sutton Trust (2011) *Degree of success: university chances by individual school*, London: The Sutton Trust.

The Guardian (2011) 'Will design and technology survive the curriculum review?', 5 April. Available at: www.guardian.co.uk/education/2011/apr/05/james-dyson-design-technology

Tönnies, F. (1887) Gemeinschaft und Gesellschaft, Leipzig: Fues's Verlag. (Translated, 1957 by Charles Price Loomis as Community and Society, East Lansing, MI: Michigan State University Press.

Unterhalter, E. (2009) 'Social justice, development theory and the question of education', in R. Cowen, A. M. Kazamias, and E. Unterhalter (eds) *International handbook of comparative education*, vol 22, Springer.

Unterhalter, E. (2012) 'Education', in S. Deneulin and L. Shahani (eds) *An introduction to the human development and capability approach: freedom*, London: Earthscan.

Van der Veer, R. and Valsiner, J. (1994) *The Vygotsky reader*, Oxford: Basil Blackwell Ltd.

Vernon, J. (2013) 'Open online courses - an avalanche that might just get stopped', *The Guardian*, 29 April, available at: www.guardian.co.uk/education/2013/apr/29/massive-open-online-courses

Vignoles, A., Galindo_Rueda, F. and Marcenaro-Gutierrez, O. (2004) 'The widening socio-economic gap in UK higher education', *National Institute Economic review*, 190: 70–82.

Vygotsky, L.S. (1978) *Mind in society: the development of higher psychological processes*, Cambridge, MA: Harvard University Press.

Vygotsky, L.S. (1986) *Thought and language* (rev. ed.), Cambridge MA: MIT Press.

Walker, M. (2005) Amartya Sen's capability approach and education, *Educational Action Research*, 13(1):103–110.

Walker, M. and Unterhalter, E. (2007) 'The capability approach: its potential for work in education', in M. Walker and E. Unterhalter (eds) *Amartya Sen's capability approach and social justice in education*, New York, NY: Palgrave Macmillan.

Wertsch, J. (1991) *Voices of the mind; a sociocultural approach to mediated action*, London: Harvester.

Wheelahan, L. (2010) *Why knowledge matters in the curriculum, a social realist argument*, New York, NY: Routledge.

Wilkins, R. (2011) *Research engagement for school development*, London: Institute of Education, University of London.

Wolf, A. (2011) *Review of vocational education – the Wolf report*, London: DfE.

Young, M. (2007) *Bringing knowledge back in: From social constructivism to social realism in the sociology of education*, London: Routledge.

Young, M. (2008) 'From constructivism to realism in the sociology of the curriculum', *Review of Research in Education*, 32(1): 1–28.

Young, M. (2009) 'What are schools for?', in H. Daniel, J. Lauder, J. Porter (eds) *Knowledge, values and educational policy*, London: Routledge, pp 10–18.

Young, M. (2011) 'The return to subjects: A sociological perspective on the UK coalition government's approach to the 14–19 curriculum', *Curriculum Journal*, 22(2): 265-278.

Young, M. (2013) 'Overcoming the crisis in curriculum theory: a knowledge-based approach', *Journal of Curriculum Studies*, 45(2): 101–18.

Young, M. and Muller, J. (2010) 'Three educational scenarios for the future: lessons from the sociology of knowledge', *European Journal of Education*, 45(1): Part I.

Index

NOTE: Page numbers followed by *n* refer to information in a note.